VERMEER

PASCAL BONAFOUX

VERMEER

KONECKY&KONECKY

Frontispiece
Girl Interrupted at Her Music
Oil on canvas. 39.3 x 44.4 cm.
The Frick Collection, New York

Konecky & Konecky
150 Fifth Ave.
New York, N Y 10011

Documentation, commentaries and captions by Lorraine Levy
with the assistance of Valérie Pénicaut.

ISBN: 1-56852-308-4

Vermeer
and His Time

Johannes Vermeer was born in Delft in October of 1632. He was baptized on October 31. He died in 1675 on either December 13 or 14 and was buried two days later in a tomb in the Old Church of Delft. These dates and a few other passing references are the only documentary testimony to his life. The rest is a matter of doubt and speculation. If one holds to the dictionary definition of biography as a genre of writing that has for its main object the history of a particular life, it is clear that a biography of Vermeer is impossible. Or an imposture. Or one has to accept that it consists of one thing only: his painting.

A witness: May 14, 1669, Pieter Teding van Berckhout, a rich young country squire, noted in his journal: "I awoke this morning, spoke to my cousin Brasser from Brile and walked over to Delft to see Zuijlechem van der Horst and Nieuwpoort. Arriving there I met an excellent painter named Vermeer, who showed me some unusual work he had done." He writes again on June 21: "I wrote to my cousin Barckhout who lives in Brile and then went out to see the celebrated painter Vermeer who showed me some

examples of his art. The most extraordinary thing about them is his use of perspective." This is one of the only two contemporary descriptions of the painter's work. One has to look to archives for any other mention of him.

In regards to these archives, on April 23, 1653, a certain Balthens set down before a notary a claim for the sum of 1,500 florins that he was owed for some goods. Vermeer countersigned as a witness. He was twenty years old. The document does not mention that he was a painter.

Eight months later on December 29, 1653, Johannes Vermeer became a member of the Guild of Saint Luke in Delft. He was only able to pay 1-1/2 florins of the 6 florin initiation fee at this time. It was not until July of 1656 that he made good on the outstanding debt.

January 10, 1654: "Jan Vermeer, master painter" was witness to a document that noted a debt of 500 florins owed by the widow of an auctioneer, named Joost Pietersz. At the end of April in same year he was once again witness to a debt this time before the notary Govert Rota, who did not find it necessary to state that he was a painter.

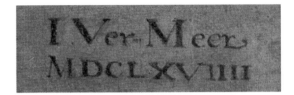

Before the same notary on December 14, 1655, "Sr. Johannes Reijnijersz. Vermeer" and his wife were the guarantors for a debt of 250 florins contracted by the painter's father.

November 30, 1657: "Johannis Reynierszoon Vermeer" and his wife Catharina Bolnes borrowed 200 florins from Pieter Claesz. van Ruijven, payable in one year at a rate of 4.5%. No word of his painting.

In May of 1667, Maria Thins gave her son-in-law the right to recover debts in her name. By this act she permitted him to take whatever steps he deemed necessary to protect her interests, including the sale of her possessions. Fragmentary notices that serve only to confirm that he was a painter: "Johannis Vermeer, master painter," "Sr. Johannes Reijijersz. Vermeer, master painter," "Johannis Reynierszoon Vermeer, painter." Nothing more.

"Johannis Reynierszoon Vermeer." The pastor Taurinius who so baptized him on October 31, 1632, at the New Reform Church bore the same Christian name. Witnessing the event were Pieter Brammer, Jan Heijndricxz. and Maertge Jans. His father Reynier was forty-one years old at the time, his mother Digna Baltens, about thirty-seven. They had named their son after his grandfather Jan, who was a tailor. Catholic families as well as the leading Calvinists preferred the Latin form, Johannis or Joannis, which seemed more elegant. As an adult, the painter used only the form Johannes. And he never used his patronymic, Reynierszoon, "son of Renier" when signing his work. *The Art of Painting* is signed on the border behind the neck of the model, the letters clear in the margin: I Ver Meer.

The Geographer, is signed in the same fashion. The date MDCLXVIIII, 1669, lies under the signature. This is one of the few times the artist has added a date, and there is some doubt about the authenticity of the work. *A Girl Asleep* is signed. I Vmeer can be seen under the picture frame that hangs above the girl's head. And like the signature in *Street in Delft* under the closed window on the left, it is in brown letters. In *Woman with a Pearl Necklace*, as in *The Love Letter*, as on the door of the armoire behind the *Astronomer*, the letters "I, V and M" are interlaced in a kind of monogram with the letters "eer" running off to the right. The *View of Delft* is only signed, on the ship at the bottom left, with a monogram. Whatever form it takes, the artist's signature does not include his father's name. But there is little to deduce from this singular manner of signing.... Jan Jansz. Treck signed his work "J Treck," Jan Jansz. van de Velde signed his "J. van de Velde fecit," and Jan Davidsz. de Hem signed his "Johannes de Heem fecit." These are simply examples of contemporary painters who had the same Christian name as Vermeer. None mention their father's name. We should not therefore deduce that his avoidance of the use of his father's name constituted a rejection of his father.

There are no examples of Vermeer's father's name being mentioned with the title "Monsieur," "Signor" or "de eerbare" (a Dutch title of respect), nor is it preceded by the letters "Sr" for "signor" or "seigneur" as is the case with Vermeer's own name in the document notarized by Govert Rota in 1655, where Vermeer is titled "Sr. Johannes Reijnijersz. Vermeer." Vermeer did

not have to be silent about his father's name to protect his own reputation. His father did not carry the name Vermeer. His surname was not inherited.

Reynier Jansz., who married Digna Baltens in Amsterdam in 1615, was inscribed as a citizen of Delft under the name Reynier Vos or Reynier Van der Minne, on October 13, 1631, at the Guild of Saint Luke, as a dealer in works of art. A document of the same year establishes that he owned an auberge on the Voldersgracht under the sign of *Die Vliegende Vos*, the Flying Fox. When their lease was up, the Reynier family left the Voldersgracht, for the Market Place and the Auberge Mechelen. Vermeer's father purchased it for 2,700 florins. He put 200 florins down. The rest was secured by two notes payable at 5%, one in the amount of 2,100 florins to a brewer in Haarlem and the second for 400 florins to a certain Arent Jorisz. Pynacker of Delft. This meant that his mortgage payments totaled about 125 florins per year, less than his rent at the Flying Fox. To get a sense of how much money this was, one need consider that a doctor on the municipal payroll had an annual income of 1,500 to 2,000 florins, a professor received somewhat less, perhaps 1,200 per annum. A ship's carpenter could expect an income of about 100 florins. Actors, on the other hand, were not paid much more than two florins for each performance, and yet they had little to complain of, seeing how stage hands made only one sixth of that amount. Another point that we need to bear in mind is that the florin of this time did not have a unique established value. The florin of Holland differed from that of Zwolle, which was not that of Kampen, nor that of Deventer. Different currencies were used as media of exchange: crowns, cavaliers, ducats, etc. And one last point, the florin, which did not officially become the coin of the realm in the Netherlands until 1694, had been continually sinking in value during the pre-

ceding century and a half. The florin of 1681 was worth only one half of that of 1544.

On February 17, 1638, Willem de Langue, a notary, registered the last will and testament of Vermeer's parents. Its disposition was reciprocal; each signatory would inherit the estate and the debts of the other. Johannes and his sister Gertruijt, called Gertruy, who was born in 1620, are mentioned only as the "child or children." Johannes's name is passed over in silence. Silence once again....

All we know is that Johannes lived at the Flying Fox on the Voldersgracht and then on the Market Place at the Auberge Mechelen. Nothing more.

Nor do we have any indication of how or where Johannes learned to paint. For admission in the Guild of Saint Luke, the candidate was required to undergo an apprenticeship for six years with one or several masters. Who taught Vermeer his craft? Was it Cornelius Daemen Rietwijck or Leonaert Bramer, or d'Evert van Aelst or Carel Fabritius? Fabritius was ten years older than Vermeer and arrived in Delft in 1650. But he was not entered onto the rolls of the Guild until fourteen months prior to Vermeer. Now, as no one except guild members were permitted to have students, it does not seem possible that Fabritius could have been Vermeer's teacher.

And how could Reynier Jansz., who had to pay a yearly mortgage of 125 florins, afford to pay an extra 50 florins per year, the cost of the first two years of an apprentice's training? With food and lodging near a teacher in Amsterdam or Utrecht, the next four years could easily cost double that. Admission into the studios of the most celebrated teachers, Abraham Bloemart

for example, could cost as much as 100 florins a year, and to that had to be added the cost of bed and board. Was business at the Flying Fox and the Auberge Mechelen good enough to allow Johannes to receive an education of this sort? There is little indication that his father's business as an art dealer was flourishing. In 1623, Reynier Jansz. handed over to his father-in-law, Balthasar Claes Gerrits, sixteen paintings as collateral for a loan. The inventory mentions a *Sacrifice of Abraham* valued at 1-1/2 florins, a *Portrait of his Excellency the Prince Maurits and Prince Hendrick* worth 4 florins and a brothel scene estimated at 3 florins. The total value of all sixteen paintings was appraised at 53.5 florins. What works was Vermeer's father selling twenty or twenty-five years later? What painters was the future artist exposed to in his parents home? Perhaps his apprenticeship never took him outside of Delft.

What of Amsterdam? There is no real evidence to prove that Vermeer ever visited it. In 1654 or perhaps 1656, he painted *Christ in the House of Mary and Martha*. In 1650 or perhaps 1651, Erasmus Quellinus painted the same subject. The citizens of Amsterdam had commissioned an allegorical work on a grand scale to hang in the Town Hall.

In Vermeer's painting, Christ's left hand rests on the arm of his chair as does the hand of Christ in the painting by Quellinus. But that the same pose is struck in both paintings does not constitute proof that Vermeer owed his composition to Quellinus. It is true that behind the seated Mary, whose head rests on her left wrist, Vermeer has painted a series of open doors, and Quellinus, as well, shows us an open door behind Mary. Yet though the perspectives are similar, this still cannot pass for proof.

The right hand of Christ who is responding to Martha is slightly raised and points at Mary. Though this motif is also found in Quellinus's work, there is still not enough here to confirm any relationship with certainty. There is certainly more divergence here than between Rembrandt's painting *Balaam's Ass*, which he signed in 1626 with the monogram "RL", and that of his teacher Lastman on the same theme. The differences between these paintings of Vermeer and Quellinus are in fact essential ones. In the latter's, Martha stands with her back facing the left; in the former's, she is standing behind a table on which she places a loaf of bread in a basket. This simple basket stands in stark contrast to the turkeys, ducks, pigeons, meats, artichokes and bunches of asparagus that fill up the left side of the Quellinus painting. Martha has a broom in her hand and points to them.

These are the words of Saint Luke (x: 41-42), which both of these paintings illustrate: "Martha, Martha, thou art careful and troubled about many things: But one thing is needful; and Mary hath chosen that good part, which shall not be taken away from her." The lowered eyes of Martha as painted by Vermeer signify acquiescence. In the painting of Quellinus, Martha stretches out her hand in the reproach she makes to Christ in the preceding verse: "Lord, dost thou not care that my sister hath left me to serve alone? Bid her therefore that she help me." An essential difference. Quellinus paints a dialogue; Vermeer a silence of his own making. Beyond the Scriptures.

Silence once again in his painting *Diana and Her Companions*, completed in 1654 or perhaps

1656. Diana is seated on a rock and does not speak a word. Nor do her companions. The one who stands behind her contemplates the humble gesture of the figure who kneels before the goddess and washes her feet.

In 1648, Jacob van Loo had painted a similar Diana surrounded by followers. One of them, at the right, is questioning her, pointing with her index finger. And behind her two young women seem to be talking.

Jacob van Loo, just as Jan van de Noordt and Jacob Backer, worked in Amsterdam as "history painters." They worked on sacred and profane subjects. Like Quellinus, they painted episodes from the Bible and classical mythology. Their paintings buzz with speech, rumor and noise. Vermeer had already begun to express the silence of history.

Another silence: testimony from 1672 does not prove whether Vermeer ever traveled to Italy.

"Johannes Jordaen and Johannes Vermeer, eminent painters of Delft," were called to appear in front of the notary Pieter van Swieten in The Hague, at the request of the painter Hendrick Fromentiou to assess the worth of twelve Italian paintings. Faced with these purported Titians, Raphaels and Giorgiones, the two painters declared that "far from being valuable Italian paintings, they are of no value whatsoever, in fact

they are execrably done and worth about one tenth of the price asked for them." This is the only trace we have of Vermeer's ideas on painting. Not even a scrap of paper exists. We have statements by Rubens, Poussin and even a few attributed to Rembrandt. But from Vermeer, not a word.

Vermeer had probably been asked to render judgment on these paintings because he had been elected as syndic of the Guild of Saint Luke for the second time the preceding year. This guild, like all others, regulated the conduct of its members. And, as other guilds, it united different professions. There were six syndics: two makers of glass, two faience artists and two painters. This fact would not have raised eyebrows in a country where the apothecaries sold spices and wine, and the art dealers were innkeepers. The notary who set down the appraisal referred to Vermeer as an "eminent painter of Delft." This title, written in the plural, referred as well to Johannes Jordaen, who had spent some years in Italy. Ten years earlier at the end of 1662, Vermeer had been elected *hoofdman*, director of this same guild. It can't be said for certain that the election was in recognition of his merit as a painter, even though he was the youngest person in quite some time to have been so honored. Over the years, Cornelis Rietwijck, Anthony Palamedes and Leonaert Bramer were all elected syndics as were Pieter Bronckhorst and Willem Poij and other painters that time has forgotten. Painters moved away from Delft. Though Cornelis de Man returned and reestablished himself in the city, many others were never heard from again. Pieter de Hooch, Willem van Aelst, Emanuel de Witte, Jan Steen, Adam Pijnacker all ended up in The Hague or in Amsterdam.

Perhaps the recognition that Vermeer received with his election as syndic on October 18, the day dedicated to Saint Luke, patron saint of painters, had to do with the fact that he was going to execute a portrait of the Virgin. For this reason the guild members considered him a "history painter." In his *Shilderboeck*, a work published in 1694, Carel van Mander explained painting in the hierarchical terms that were so popular during this era. And history painting was placed at the summit of this hierarchy.

History painting: The reputation that Vermeer acquired as a history painter prevailed over the resistance that must have been provoked by his conversion to Catholicism. Apparently, he converted shortly before his marriage. It is likely that he had not yet been received into the church on April 5, 1653, when the engagement party gathered before the notary, Johannes Ranck. Present were Johannes Rijniersz. Vermeer and his fiancé, Catharina Bolnes, and Trijntgen Reijniers. A Captain Melling, "about 59 years old" and Leonaert Bramer, "about 58 years old," stood as witnesses testifying that they had heard Maria Thins, the mother of the bride-to-be, announce that "she would allow the banns to be made public," and repeat several times "that she would do nothing to hinder the upcoming betrothal." Is it because the family of her son-in-law was Protestant and kept an inn that she was initially reticent? Whatever her reasons, on the day before, she had refused to sign the official registry declaring the engagement. Vermeer must have converted a few days later, since the marriage was held two weeks after the publication of the marriage banns, on April 20, in the Church at Schipluy.

One hour's journey from Delft, Schipluy was a Catholic community. Father Wynants, a Jesuit priest, said the mass. The Netherlands at this time was a country that had recently fought for its independence against the Catholic monarchy of Spain; it was a country where Calvinism had acquired the status and force of a state religion. Catholic holidays, even secularized ones such as the Feast of the Three Kings, Mardi Gras and Saint Nicholas Day, were still not celebrated by the populace at large. To be Catholic here was to be tolerated, nothing more. In the Protestant town of Delft, there were only two Catholic churches. And these churches were housed in buildings that blended in with their surroundings. They did not even display a cross. In a house next to that of Vermeer's mother-in-law on the Oude Langendijck, mass was held by Jesuits. In a house of the beguines of Old Delft, Jansenism was the order of the day. Jesuit or Jansenist, the Holy Roman Apostolic church had to remain almost hidden. Despite all of this, in 1672 (or 1674) Vermeer announced his faith on canvas in what may have been his last painting.

The sphere of glass that hangs from the ceiling in *The Allegory of the Faith* and the crucifix resting on the table were perhaps inspired by an engraving representing faith in the *Emblemata Sacra de Fide, Spe, Charitate*, a book published in 1636 by the Jesuit Willem Hesius. Perhaps....

The Allegory of the Faith as painted by Vermeer owes at least as much to works written on religion as to those about painting. To paint a work symbolizing "the universal Catholic Faith" he must have had recourse to Ripa's *Iconology or a New Interpretation of Several Images*. In the form of a dictionary of allegorical figures, this

treatise presented a concept of the image in which gestures are symbols, expressions emblematic and colors attributes. It first appeared in Rome in 1604. Engravings were used as *aide-memoires* for each vice, virtue, temperament and passion. It was translated into Dutch and published in 1644 in Amsterdam. Ripa describes "the universal Catholic Faith" as "symbolized by a seated women clothed in white and holding a chalice in her right hand which she looks at attentively...." In another place Ripa describes Faith as "clothed in a sky-blue garment." Vermeer's Faith is clothed in blue and white. Ripa adds: "Under an angular rock, a serpent lies crushed.... At her side is an apple, the cause of our sin." In the painting an apple with a bite taken out of it rolls across the tiled floor and a snake lies in the corner with blood pouring out its mouth. Hanging on the wall, framed in black, is a crucifix. Ripa goes on to say that Faith should be accompanied by the figure of "Abraham sacrificing his son." Jesus on the cross is like Isaac, the son sacrificed by his father. For the sacrifice of the Old Testament, Vermeer substitutes that of the New. This was another way, perhaps, of affirming one's Catholicism in a country that since 1637 had possessed its own official translation of Scripture, commissioned by order of the Synod of Dordogne of 1618. Again referring to Ripa's description of Faith as having the world at her feet, Vermeer's figure has her right foot resting on a globe.

lies a book by Adriaen Metius on the study and observation of the stars. And on the left-hand page Vermeer has depicted in exact detail the astrolabe that Metius invented. His rendering is so precise that one can say with certainty that it was modeled on the second edition of the work, which was published in 1621. But this identification tells us nothing important about Vermeer. That we recognize some of the maps in the background or the edition of the book he has painted attests to his scrupulousness, but not his unique gifts. In *Summer or the Five Senses*, Sebastien Stoskopff painted a musical score resting open on the neck of a lute. Here the painting is detailed enough to establish that it is the 76th psalm as set to music by Claude the Younger.

Vermeer's scrupulous precision has a double-edged effect. In one sense, it establishes an undeniable credibility for the artist, and yet at the same time it is a kind of sleight-of-hand. The care with which Vermeer renders the figure who reads Adriaen Metius's treatise and examines the astrolabe that Metius invented establishes that he is unmistakably an astronomer. Yet we are not privy to his thoughts or know precisely what it is that he is studying. Vermeer's precision turns out to be a diversion; it denudes his figures of everything they have to say, and everything that can be said about them. What remains is sanded down, almost plucked bare. We are left with almost no trace of the subject's character. Ultimately his scrupulous precision is a ruse.

The same globe lies on the armoire in Vermeer's *Geographer*. It was constructed by the cartographic firm of Hondius. The *Astronomer* is pictured resting his thumb and index finger on it. He is looking up. On the tapestry in front of him,

And yet there are no hard and fast rules with Vermeer's paintings. *The View of Delft* can serve as an example. He paints the city at the point where the River Schie widens, forming a kind of river basin. We see a stone bridge. To the left is

the Schiedam Gate to which the name Kethelpoort is still applied. A certain Diederick van Bleyswijk noted in 1667 that it was "an ancient construction," and on it was a "bell tower that the boatmen used to guide themselves." To the right stands the Rotterdam Gate, which extends in a kind of gallery to the other side of the canal. Watch towers with pointed roofs rise above the surrounding buildings. On the quay, different kinds of vessels can be seen. To the left is a boat used for towing ships laden with freight, much like the ones tied up at the foot of the Rotterdam Gate. Just in front is a water coach used to carry passengers up and down the river. To the right are larger ships. Two flat-bottomed boats are of the kind used to transport herring. Behind the Rotterdam Gate, seen in bright sunlight, rises the steeple of the New Church. On the left, behind the Schiedam Gate, stand ramparts, dark brown in the shadows. They enclose densely foliated trees and a mass of red roof tops, punctuated by windows and gables. These buildings cannot be found in the street plan of Delft designed by Johannes de Ram, sometime between 1675–1678. Nor were they standing fourteen years before when Vermeer painted this panoramic scene. And this is not his only departure from strict fidelity to the town's topography. The wall between the fore-gate and the Rotterdam Gate can be found on the same plan by de Ram, and on a drawing by Jan de Bisschop as well. But there, it is perpendicular to the Schiedam Gate, while Vermeer paints it at an angle. In addition, the spire of the New Church was in reality taller and more slender than Vermeer's depiction of it. There is little doubt that Vermeer painted this scene from nature, but that does not mean that his work is merely an inventory of what lay before him.

The same furnishings and accessories appear in canvas after canvas. Against an almost unchanging background. The same wooden ceiling beams, neither painted nor adorned in any way, are seen in the room where a music lesson is being held and in the darkened room in which sits the model for *The Allegory of the Faith*. The same square porcelain tiles serve as a floor molding in *Young Woman Seated at a Virginal*, *The Letter* and *The Geographer*. White tiles without elaborate motifs are found in the background of *Young Woman Seated at a Virginal* and *Maidservant Pouring Milk*. These tiles were probably manufactured in Delft. The city was famous for them. In the eastern part of town there were ceramic factories that employed as many as twenty workers.

The room in which a young woman brings a glass to her lips in the presence of a well-dressed gentleman is paved with dark red and black floor tiles. The same tiles are found in a room in which a young woman with a silly grin is allowing a gentleman to pour her a drink. The windows admitting light into both rooms are half-open. The design of the leaded panes is the same. The same central motif; the same oval shape; the same armorial bearings. (They belonged to Janetge Jacobsdr. Vogel, the wife of Moses van Nederveen, a Delft aristocrat who died in 1624. There is pictured the figure of a woman. She holds a bridle in her right hand, indicating that she stands for Temperance.)

There is a panel of red leather, interworked with gold embroidery, set up behind the ebony crucifix that sits on a table in *The Allegory of the Faith*. It rests against the frame of a painting of the Crucifixion. The same leather panel crops up once again between the column and the door frame in *The Love Letter*, though here it lies horizontally against a wall.

A white pitcher with a tin lid sits on a table on which a drowsy maid rests her elbows. It is no different from the one that sits on a silver platter in *The Music Lesson*. It is the same one that the gentleman holds in *Lady and Gentleman Drinking Wine*. And it appears yet again, this time on a white napkin, in *Lady with Two Gentlemen*.

The painter in *The Art of Painting* wears stockings that are rolled up around his calves and a beret on his head. There is nothing extraordinary here. The same can be said of his doublet. The young man who raises a glass to the viewer in *The Procuress* holds a glass in his left hand and a kind of guitar in his right. He wears the same beret and the same doublet. From canvas to canvas the same objects, the same inventory always.

Or almost the same. Our inventory has to be thorough. (An inventory that becomes more complete as each new canvas repeats the ones that have gone before or rather creates a space wherein furnishings and accessories seem practically immutable and men and women absolutely still.) We have to start by taking this inventory. It is an exacting task. It has to be done conscientiously, paying attention to every detail; for that is the only way we can grasp what is essential. I think of Rilke's total responsiveness to the work of Cézanne, and the demands he placed upon himself when writing of this master's paintings and drawings. His words had to be "facts, objectively deduced from the works themselves."

In *A Girl Asleep*, a housemaid leans her elbows on a table covered by an Oriental tapestry. It is the same carpet as the one on which Martha places a basket of bread in *Christ in the House of Mary and Martha*. The same design with the red border behind Mary and in front of the overturned glass. The same ochre trim. But the colors of the tapestry are different in each painting.

One finds the same chair with the lions' heads in *A Girl Asleep, Woman Reading a Letter* (both the Amsterdam and Dresden paintings), *Soldier and Laughing Girl, Lady with Two Gentlemen, Young Woman with a Water Jug, The Music Lesson* and *The Letter*. In four of these canvases (*A Girl Asleep, Woman Reading a Letter* (Dresden), *Soldier and Laughing Girl,* and *The Letter*), the backs of the chairs are decorated with the same diamond-shaped devices. And they are covered in blue velvet in *Woman Reading a Letter* (Amsterdam) and *The Music Lesson*. Sometimes they are partially hidden, or turned away from the viewer, or covered with fabric.

In *The Music Lesson*, a viola da gamba rests on the ground between a chair and the red dress of a young woman standing in front of a keyboard. It is similar to one in another Vermeer painting where it leans against a virginal on which a young woman dressed in blue is playing. This viola da gamba has six strings. (The position of the other prevents us from making out how many strings it has.) From 1675 on, the viola da gamba normally had seven strings. The various keyboards in Vermeer's paintings are sloped toward the left. This kind of construction was favored by Dutch and Flemish manufacturers. On the under side of the keyboard's lid in *The Music Lesson*, a Latin inscription speaks of the virtues of music. The lids of the virginals which the young women, one standing, one seated, play, as well as the one in the *Concert*, are decorated with landscapes. Only the trees and clouds are different. The young woman with her eyes raised to the mirror facing her, as she ties a pearl necklace around her neck, wears a mantle of satin fringed with white fur. As does the seated woman holding a letter in her hand who turns toward her servant. As does another woman who is writing a letter. As does another who, seated at a table, turns towards a servant who is holding a letter out to her. As another

who plays the guitar, and another who plays the lute. As does another who holds a balance with its scales in equilibrium between her thumb an index finger.... The same satin mantle edged with fur. Though in some paintings it is dappled with black marks, as if it were ermine, and in others it is pure white. And though in every other painting the mantle is yellow, it is blue in *Woman Holding a Balance*.

In *Soldier and Laughing Girl*, a map is hanging on the wall. The same map hangs behind the lady in blue who is reading a letter. The same map is present, at a slant, on the right, in front of the doorway in *The Love Letter*. The Latin inscription, *Nova et accurata totius hollandiae west-frisiaeq topographia*, informs us that the map is of Holland and West Friesland. Published by Willem Jansz. Blaeu, it was drawn by Balthazar Florisz. van Berkenrode in 1620. In another canvas, the colors of the map have changed.

In *The Concert*, two paintings are hanging on the wall, a landscape and a genre scene. One canvas hangs on the wall in *Young Woman Standing at a Virginal*, the same genre painting.... It is *The Procuress* by Dirck van Baburen. The old woman with her hand out wants the coin that the man is holding poised above the breasts of a prostitute who is laughing and is looking backward. In *The Concert*, the picture is framed in dark wood, perhaps ebony; in *Young Woman Standing at a Virginal*, it is in a gilded frame.

A picture hangs on the back wall in *The Astronomer*. In *The Letter,* a large painting is hanging on the back wall. In the lower left of each of these pictures within a picture, we can see the same nude back of a man leaning on his right arm, which is stretched out on the ground. The same woman, with a hand held against her chest, stands above him, and farther to the right, there is another woman, dressed in somber colors. She is seated and seems to be handing an infant to another woman, who is unclothed and seated on

a rock. In *The Astronomer*, the picture is cut off, so that we cannot see below the knees of the young man who is no doubt getting out of the water. In *The Letter*, the reeds and rushes are turned to the left in front of his knee and behind his thigh. There is little doubt that this painting represents the finding of Moses. The two canvases have different formats, but they are the same picture. In *Young Woman Standing at a Virginal*, Cupid, framed in ebony, holds up a playing card that cannot be identified. (Though that should not be surprising. Love is a card that one takes by chance.) The left leg of this *putto* is gracefully bent. This leg is hidden by the man bent over the sheet of music which he holds out to the young woman in *A Girl Interrupted at Her Music*. This leg creates a diagonal line from the picture hanging on the wall to the head of the servant in *A Girl Asleep*. Near Cupid's leg is a mask. There is no mask next to his leg in the painting hanging in *Young Woman Standing at a Virginal*.

If we look at the rooms in which so many of Vermeer's paintings are set we find the same square black tiles. They are present in *The Music Lesson*, in *The Concert,* in *Young Woman Standing at a Virginal* and In *Young Woman Seated at a Virginal*, in the painting of the artist's studio, in one in which a woman reads a letter while her servant looks out the window. as well as in the room where the figure of *The Allegory of the Faith* holds her hand to her breast. In all of these rooms, the black tiles create cruciform shapes. The only exceptions are *The Music Lesson*, where the black tiles entirely surround the white tiles and *The Allegory of the Faith*, where it is the white tiles that are arranged in the form of crosses.

The same window is half-open in the room where a young woman drinks in the presence of a gentleman and in the room where another woman drinks a glass of white wine in the company of two men. And the panes form the same

design in the slightly open window in *Young Woman with a Water Jug*, as in other rooms where, though closed, the windows cast light into the interior: the room in which is set *The Music Lesson* and another room in which a music lesson is interrupted, and in one where a woman strums on a lute, and in another where a woman is tying a pearl necklace around her neck. And still the same design in the room where a woman sits writing a letter with her servant in attendance. Only that in this last canvas, the window that sheds light on the painting of Moses that is hung above the woman writing the letter is marked with blue and yellow armorial bearings. And there are other windows as well. Those that light up a young woman reading a letter, and a soldier and young woman in conversation, and the virginal in front of which a woman is standing are all the same. Or almost. The upper part of the windows are designed in diamond and trapezoid shapes above four or five rows of square panes. But in the first instance the window is wide open, in the second half-open and in the third it is shut.

And still other windows.... Those next to which an astronomer and a geographer think and ruminate. Above five rows of square panes, there are diamond and triangular ones. Molding on the right side in *The Astronomer* partly conceals an oval pane painted in green and red at the center of the window. This window may contain heraldic emblems as well.

As perhaps do the designs hidden by a curtain that falls in front of the window in *The Geographer*, despite the sash at the left that holds it.

All of Vermeer's windows, just as in the *Maidservant Pouring Milk*, are located on the left side of his paintings. From one painting to the next there is hardly any difference between them. And it is of little importance whether the windows are open, ajar or closed, whether the panes are colored or opaque. They look out onto nothing. The only thing that matters is interior space.

Some objects that are only seen once or twice in his paintings turn up again in different guises. Two months after the death of the painter, a complete inventory was taken of his household goods. It comprised paintings, furniture, clothing, even cooking utensils. The house on Oude Langendijck was thoroughly gone through, from the cellar to the attic. As far as paintings go, the inventory mentions a Christ on the cross, probably the one that appears in the *Allegory of the Faith*; "*Bas met doootshoofd*," a still life with a viola da gamba and skull, probably seen in the background of *The Letter*, and a small seascape, no doubt the one that hangs on the wall in *The Love Letter*. There are also portraits of Vermeer's mother and father, two portraits by Fabritius, ten portraits of the family of Maria Thins, Vermeer's mother-in-law, who lived with him and his wife, and two portraits by Samuel van Hoogstraten, one of which may well be the inspiration for the painting hanging on the wall in the *Lady with Two Gentlemen*.

In the *Music Lesson*, a painting with an interesting history makes an appearance. Its model was a painting that Maria Thins received in the divorce settlement from her husband Reinier Bolnes, *Schilderije van een die de borst suyght*. Perhaps it is a tableau representing Christian Charity offering her breast to feed another.

Not only paintings, but other objects as well keep reappearing. An example: Maria Thins, in her second will, in which she leaves her estate to

her daughter Catharina, Vermeer's wife, mentions among other items, a gold cross, silver plate and a vermeil pitcher for wine that the *Young Woman with a Water Jug* is no doubt holding by its handle. All of the objects in his paintings seem to have been taken from the painter's store of household goods. That does not, however, make the painter's work into some kind of intimate diary. His paintings tell no stories.

On December 15, 1675, the body of Johannes Vermeer was brought down the Oude canal to the Old Church. It was buried the following day. The register, which lists "persons who have died in the town of Delft and have been buried within the confines of the Old Church," establishes that a child of Vermeer's died on June 27, 1673 and was buried in the Vermeer family tomb. Two other children, who died at early ages, were buried there as well, one in 1667 and the other in 1669. In April of 1676, "Catharina, widow of Johannes Vermeer," declared that she had been left with eleven children. A second declaration made in 1678 indicates that at the time of the painter's death their ages ranged from one to eighteen. Two children play in the *Street in Delft*, but there is no proof that these were his own children. Two of the young women that he painted, the *Woman Reading a Letter* (in the Gemäldegalerie in Dresden) and the *Woman Holding a Balance*, are pregnant, but that does not mean that his wife modeled for either one of these paintings that date from 1662 and 1663. All the biographer is left with is more uncertainty.

Over the course of time, Vermeer has but one signature. It has several forms but does not change from year to year: V Meer, I Vmeer, I Ver Meer. Even [IVM]eer, which is written on the little stool where Mary sits listening to Christ. We see his signature on the table in front of which a young girl ties a string of pearls around her neck, on the wall behind *The Lacemaker*, as it is behind the *Young Woman Seated at a Virginal*, as in *The Love Letter*, and on the door of the bureau in *The Astronomer*, and on a piece of paper hanging off a table in *The Letter*.

These canvases were painted over a period of fifteen years. Only three of them are dated: *The Procuress*, 1656, *The Astronomer*, 1668, *The Geographer*, 1669. And the last two may have been repainted. Vermeer remains unchanging.

Works with no date. One of the only dated works is *The Procuress* (1656). It is considered one of his earliest works. *Allegory of the Faith* passes for one of his last. Some believe that it was painted in 1669, others that it must have been 1674, and others lean towards 1671 or '72 or '70.... Beginning in 1663 or 1665, Vermeer seems to have mastered the meticulous technique that van Mieris had perfected; just as he had already taken whatever he needed from van Baburen, van Loo, Fabritius, Pieter de Hooch and Nicolas Maes. White points capture the light in his *Woman Reading a Letter* and in his *Soldier and Laughing Girl*. But they are not reference points. There are no sure internal grounds on which to establish incontrovertible dates for any of Vermeer's paintings. He remains unchanging.

The models in his paintings appear and reappear like the same actors in different roles. In

front of the same bureau, the same model can be seen first as *The Astronomer* in 1668 and then as *The Geographer* in 1669 (if one can believe the dates). The model in *Maidservant Pouring Milk*, painted in 1660 or perhaps 1661, has the same high forehead, straight nose and dimpled chin as the one in *A Girl Asleep*, painted in 1667. The *Young Woman with a Water Jug*, painted in 1662, has the same sweetly rounded forehead as the *Woman Holding a Balance*, painted between 1662 and 1665. The woman who posed for *Woman with a Pearl Necklace*, painted around the same time, has a retroussé nose much like that of the girl playing the clavier in *The Concert*. Or perhaps it is because they wear the same bunch of ribbons in their hair that their profiles blend into one. The chin of the *Young Woman Standing at a Virginal*, painted in about 1670, and that of the lady in *Mistress and Maid*, painted some three years earlier, have the same shape, and the lock of blond hair that hangs loose over their foreheads is the same in each case. The *Young Woman Seated at a Virginal*, painted in 1675 or 1676, has the same round face as the model for the *Allegory of the Faith*, completed a few years before. Or perhaps it is because they wear the same mantle embroidered with gold trim that they seem to be the same person. The *Girl with a Pearl Earring* of 1665 and Clio in *The Art of Painting*, painted between 1662 and 1665, have the same ridge over their eyebrows, the same straight nose, the same slightly full lips. The same faces. Only the roles change.

Role. It is perhaps not the correct word. It suggests the theater, which is the province of genre painting. The business of anecdotes, narratives, proverbial wisdom. We know the charla-

tan flogging his shoddy goods in a Frans van Mieris painting, and what the woman tilting back in her chair is saying to the young boy standing outside the window in that of Jacob Vrel, and in Jan Jacob van Valsen's painting, we can be pretty sure what sort of fortune the old woman is relaying to the young girl whose palm lies open before her. We are familiar with the shrieks of laughter that issue forth from the taverns of Jan Steen or Adriaen van Ostade, with the whispered conversations that Gerard ter Borch depicts, and those of Gabriel Metsu. But the works of Vermeer.... What anecdotes, what domestic dramas are his?

One fact continues to trouble art critics and historians. Vermeer never painted a wholly original or unexpected scene. He paints a young woman reading a letter, as does Gerard ter Borch and Pieter de Hooch. He has a young woman putting on a necklace, but so does Frans van Mieris....

He paints men and women gathering to play music or for a music lesson, the same as Jacob van Loo, Joost van Geel and Gerard ter Borch....

Vermeer uses his studio as a subject for his painting. Just like Frans van Mieris, Adriaen van Ostade and Job Adriansz. Berckheyde. That in one of these the painter paints himself all alone and in another a visitor is looking at a painting resting on an easel does not change the facts of the matter.

Vermeer paints gestures. None of them are original, unexpected or spontaneous.

He paints a servant pouring milk into a jug. A humble domestic action. In a kitchen painted by Pieter Cornelis van Slingelandt in 1648, a young girl peels carrots. A similar domestic gesture. So also is that of the girl painted by Gerard

ter Borch in 1655. She pours water over the crossed hands of her mistress onto a plate. All are gestures which speak of everyday life. In another of Vermeer's paintings, a young woman is holding a balance. Perhaps one day when she grows old, she will look like that aged woman painted by David III Rijckaert, who weighs out her gold. Her serene smile will become a covetous sneer. The unbalanced scales that the old woman holds stand for Avarice, one of the seven deadly sins. Vermeer's young woman is the embodiment of innocence. She is pregnant and stands before a painting of the Last Judgment, in which the elect are separated from the damned. These everyday gestures have a hidden component, one that suggests moral values.

Nor are the objects that Vermeer paints exceptional in any way.

The chairs with the lions' heads that appear in many of Vermeer's paintings are similar to those that Pieter de Hooch includes in a picture of a young woman reading a letter and in another where a woman combs a child's hair. (And there also are the same square Delft tiles running along the bottom of a staircase behind them.) The same bourgeois accessories. The glass Vermeer's sleeping girl has overturned can also be found in *The Crab Dinner*, as painted by Willem Claesz. Heda in 1648. The knot of ribbons that ties up the hair of certain of Vermeer's models is identical to one worn by a young woman eating oysters in a painting by Jan Steen.

The satin mantle bordered with white fur that Vermeer dresses his models in seems to be unique. But let us look a little more closely. Metsu has painted a doctor examining a patient's urine and another of a woman eating oysters; Gerard ter Borch has painted a woman who reads a letter while the messenger who brought it waits for her answer, and another woman who plays a musical instrument for two gentlemen. All of these models wear the same kind of

mantle. That one is velvet rather than satin, that some are red, or blue, or yellow, or black, doesn't change anything. It is the same short mantle that comes down to just below the elbows, and all are bordered with white fur.

The mirror standing next to a window in a painting from the 1660s by Pieter Jansens Elinga that shows a young woman sweeping, occupies the same place as the one in Vermeer's painting, *Woman with a Pearl Necklace*. And on the tables painted by Job Adriansz. Berckheyde lie the same tapestries with their shadowy folds as those adorning Vermeer's paintings.

Vermeer paints scenes from everyday life, the same life as his contemporaries observed all around them. The clothing worn by the models, the day's fashions, are inconsequential. The objects are ordinary. Even the careful attention to detail is commonplace. Yet, on one side is Vermeer and on the other banality.

Vermeer deliberately paints these humdrum scenes and everyday objects. He paints these ordinary rooms *precisely* because of their insignificance. Their lack of distinction is the secret that lies within his mysterious canvases. Because here human purposes are adulterated, even erased. And euphemism yields to painting. Space, form and an incomparable light. These are his only subjects.

A canvas by Vermeer. Nothing happens in it. It is not trying to say anything. No words are spoken. It is simply there. That is all. Without commentary.

The Lacemaker. She is bent over her work, sure of her gestures. But who is to say what exactly it is that she is doing. We can only be sure of the quality of her concentration: precise, intense, yet serene. Her gestures are silent ones. She alone knows the secret of her labors. She is what she is doing. Totally absorbed in her task, she is almost absent. Silent.

Genre scenes tell stories of sexual conquest, lovers' stratagems, kitchen and hearth, daily matters with diverse incidents, words and noises. There is only an allusion to episodes of this kind in Vermeer. And all of the people whom he paints keep silent. A silence that is scarcely disturbed by the rustling of a garment, the scratching of a pen across a sheet of paper, the pouring of milk into a pitcher. Silence of time stretching into infinity. Silence like that of still lifes, which he did not paint. A still space. Silence of time without narrative.

*T*he Procuress. In 1656, Vermeer, who was at this point just beginning his career, painted a brothel scene. He is sure to have known the old Dutch proverb: "*Voor herberg, achter bordeel*" (In the front an inn, in the back a brothel). There can be little doubt of the intentions of the man about to drop a coin into the hand of the lady. The way he holds the coin, between his thumb and index finger, and a single open button on the lady's dress, make everything quite clear. Vermeer refused to paint the two dogs mating that can be seen in the background of a Frans van Mieris painting on the same theme. There is one anecdotal element in this painting. In the midst of the silence a joking young man raises his glass to the viewer. (Note that this is the only painting by Vermeer in which we see a man drinking.)

The stakes are similar in his painting, *Lady with Two Gentlemen,* a canvas painted five or six years later. But the tone is different. Here we find hypocrisy, etiquette and thoughtlessness blended together. Seated behind the table, resting his head on his hand, one man waits while the other achieves his purpose. Or is he sleeping off a drunk? Although there is no glass in front of him. As to the young woman it is quite clear that this is not the first glass that her companion has pressed upon her. We can tell by his shy and mocking smile, which she, silly woman, does not catch. Vermeer does not content himself with the conventional attitudes and gestures that one would find in a de Hooch painting. No words are spoken. An anecdote and then silence….

A Girl Asleep. Is it she who in her drunkenness has tipped over the glass that lies between the heavy folds of tapestry and the white pitcher with its tin lid? The same kind of pitcher appears in a merry company painted by Jan Steen in 1660. But that is the only thing the two paintings have in common. Steen depicts a man smoking a pipe and splitting his sides laughing, next to a woman in a drunken stupor, whose half-opened blouse partially reveals her breasts. The Dutch saying, "*de wijn is een spotter*" (wine is a joker), could serve as the title for this painting, as it does for an engraving by Hendrick Bary after a canvas by Frans van Lieris, painted in 1664. There, a grimacing, sniggering clown empties the contents of a chamber pot over the head of a woman passed out with drink. Vermeer shows us a young girl dozing. A glass has been overturned, but the empty glass is not necessarily the reason for her drowsiness. Perhaps it is simply fatigue. Silence without any narrative element.

The Music Lesson. Does the title really suit this work, painted in 1664? The viola de gamba lying on the floor undoubtedly belongs to the man listening to the young woman play. He has just set it down, or is just about to take it up. His face gives nothing away. He doesn't judge, correct or comment. He does not keep time with his left hand. Is this really a lesson? Nothing in the painting insists on that interpretation. *The Music Lesson* painted by Jan Steen (ca. 1659) leaves no room for doubt. A man with an attentive but vaguely condescending smile looks at a nervous and awkward young woman seated in front of a keyboard. The only common element is that the virginals, which Steen's figure stares at and Vermeer's plays, are both decorated with similar motifs of hippocampus and arabesques framing a Latin inscription. Steen's tableau tells a story. Vermeer's does not. Vermeer does not paint stories.

Rather, Vermeer paints a moment in passing time. He paints gestures in the same way as he paints the Delft sky. It has just rained, or it is about to rain. The sky is clouding over, or it is just starting to clear. There has been a recent downpour, or one is about to occur.

He paints a moment suspended between what has just occurred and what is about to occur. A hesitation. Or time itself hesitating. That which was happening has been interrupted and in a moment will begin again.

And this suspended moment is a kind of detour. That which preceded it did not necessarily bring it about. That which succeeds it will not necessarily develop out of it. The moment stands in relation to the course of time as a broken or refracted line. A halt. In *The Astronomer*, the scientist raises his eyes from the open book towards the celestial globe. For verification, for reflection? From book to globe. They are part of the same ongoing course of study.

An interruption. A geographer stops looking at the map he has been consulting. What is he thinking about? What disturbs his concentration? Voices heard from outside his window, a conversation, a cry, laughter? Compass in hand, he is about to resume his labors. But the painted gesture is one of displacement.

The painted gesture is displaced.... As if unexpected or the product of a sudden deviation. Vermeer's precisely painted gestures are filled with ambiguity. Without consequences, or perhaps simply indecipherable. A servant holds a letter while her mistress sits at a table. Is she about to hand it over to her, or has she just received it? Why does the young woman holding in her left hand the handle of a pitcher raise her right hand to the window? Is she about to open it or close it? What is the pregnant woman who stands in front of a table with an open jewelry box weighing in the balance she is holding? It is not that these gestures have no meaning. It is simply that they tell us nothing.

Or almost nothing. Or something that is not seen, known or heard. And that changes nothing.... The letters that one woman reads in

front of an open window and another woman holds in front of a map hanging on a wall exist only as a thickness of paper. One of the women is pregnant, the other is not. But for both, their serenity amounts to indifference. What is it that they are reading that leaves them so unmoved?

Children are kneeling in the street. What games are they playing? What rolling object or scurrying insect are they following so attentively along the sidewalk pavement? The solution remains invisible.

Gestures toward the invisible. Like the yellow ribbon of the pearl necklace that a young woman is tying around her neck. Like the words other women write while their maids attend them. Like the work over which the lacemaker stoops. All invisible in the same calm light.

A light that seems made of the same substance as shadow. There is no line of demarcation separating light and shadow. Light degrades quietly until it becomes shadow. Light and shadow play over tapestries, walls, human features. Light that is nothing other than paint.

Vermeer has left no drawings and no engravings. And just as he paints genre scenes that have no narrative content, he paints portraits devoid of personality. His genre scenes tell no stories; his portraits are of no one.

Women's faces. Young women. The pose one strikes is same as that of another. Their heads are turned in three-quarter view. They face the viewer over their left shoulder. A fleeting smile. One's mouth is slightly open; the other's lips are tightly pressed together. One wears a blue and yellow turban. The fringed border of a yellow scarf knotted at the top of her head falls to her shoulders. The other's scarf is a more muted yellow. It is bound up with her chignon and descends at an angle down the middle of her back. One wears a white collar around her neck; the irregular triangle of the other's collar is partially hidden by her gray satin wrap. And hanging from their earlobes, the same pearl, the same drop of light.

Number 38 in the sale catalog of the auction held in Amsterdam on May 16, 1696 mentions, "*Een tronie in Antique klederen ongemeen konstig.*" (A head in antique costume skillfully painted.) The word *trone*, meaning head, had a distinct technical denotation. It referred to paintings of models dressed in turbans or other Eastern garb to evoke some hazy legend or some hazy notion of the Orient. The precise locale did not matter very much. Wherever it was, the Dutch East India Company was certain to have traveled and done business there. (The Company had an office in Delft, one of five in Holland.) Van Mander writing in his artist's handbook, the *Shilderboeck,* published in 1604, asserts that "history painting" is the highest form of art. Portraiture is somewhat looked down upon.

"*Conterfeyten nae t'leven*" (to paint a portrait from life) was regarded as a less accomplished form of art. But the *trone* was more acceptable. It was not regarded as portraiture but subsumed into the genre of history painting. That still does not convince us that Vermeer dressed his models in scarves and turbans to evoke the Orient. And what of the pearls that dangle from their earlobes? What are they meant to suggest?

A painter, his arm resting on a support, holds his brush towards a crown of laurels sketched out on the canvas in front of him. His back is turned to the spectator. Just as working painters had to be familiar with van Mander's *Shilderboeck,* so they were expected to have read Cesare Ripa's *Iconologia.* No doubt Vermeer had come across the following description: "*Een magdeken met ee lauwerkrans, die in der rechterhand een Trompethoud en mette linker een boek waarop bovenop geschreven zal ziln: 'Thucydides'. Dese muse is Clio...*" (A young woman crowned with laurels, who holds a trumpet in her right hand and in her left a book on which is written the name "Thucydides".) Vermeer is conscientious. He follows Ripa in every detail. His model holds a trumpet in her right hand and a book in her left. Perhaps the first book of history ever written: *The History of the Pelopennesian Wars* by Thucydides. The model's left sleeve falls over the book cover so that we cannot read the title. But there is no doubt that it is History herself and not one of her surrogates who poses here.

The model stands in front of a wall on which a map hangs. A chandelier partially hides an inscription in capital letters: *Nova XVII provinciarum Germniae inferoris descriptio et accurata earundem...de novo emendata...rectissime edita per Nicolaum Piscatorem.* Jacob Ochtervely and Nicloas Maes included this same map in canvases that they painted. It was published in 1635 by Nicolas Vissher (whose name in Latin becomes *Piscator*). This map, which is torn vertically down the middle, does not take into account the establishment of the Dutch Republic. The northern and southern provinces are shown as still one unified country. On January 30, 1648, the Peace of Westphalia definitively established the independence of the United Provinces. It comprised the seven provinces of the northern part of the Netherlands: Holland, Utrecht, Zeeland, Guilder, Friesland, Overijssel and Groningen. A general assembly was held in The Hague in 1651 in the great room of the Binnenhof decorated with flags seized from the Spanish enemy. The result reinforced the unity of the country. The ten Catholic provinces of the South, formally incorporated by the Union of Arras on January 6, 1579, remained under the control of the Spanish monarchy. This map follows seventeenth-century conventions—north is to the right and west above. Views of different towns ornament the edges of the map. Smaller towns such as Groningen and Deventer are shown, but oddly enough Delft is absent.

There are no candles in the chandelier that hangs in front of this map. Two wings are spread under its circular framework, and two heads face each other. The chandelier painted in 1617 by Jan Brueghel the Elder and Peter Paul Rubens on the ceiling of a cabinet of curiosities is not much different from this one. A similar double-headed eagle surmounts it. And the one which Lucas of Leyden engraved under his portrait of Maximillian I has the same wings spread out like palm leaves. The Hapsburg eagle....

Perhaps this eagle with two heads represents a nostalgia for the days of the Holy Roman Empire, that empire over which Charles V had reigned and that at his abdication had encompassed the Netherlands, Franche-Comté, Castille and its American territories, Aragon and its Italian dependencies, Sardinia, Sicily and the Kingdom of Naples, and the hereditary German possessions of the Hapsburg dynasty. With the departure of Charles, this empire had gradually begun to fall apart.

And is the tear that runs through the middle of the map that hangs on the wall a political metaphor for the partition of the Netherlands?

In the triangle defined by the trumpet, the book and the muse's forearm, one can see the view of T'Hof van Hollandt, the seat of government at The Hague. On the opposite side of the map lies T'Hof van Brabant, the center of government for the southern Catholic provinces. Might Clio be pointing at the north, because through war and diplomacy it had just been making history. And does the inset of T'Hof van Brabant, at which the artist's support is pointing, signify the faith of one who paints the immobility of History in turbulent times? All are questions to which we have no answers. The figure of History who poses for Vermeer is not defined by a nation or a treaty. She is not a particular series of events or the account of them. She is no more the Pelopennesian War of Thucydides than she is the war that gave birth to the Dutch Republic. Here are the features of a woman with downcast eyes, enhaloed with light. A silence prevails: a silence of acquiescence and attention, patience and modesty. A silence that is barely disturbed by the friction of a paintbrush on canvas. The silence of Vermeer.

In the days following the death of Vermeer, the *Camer van Charitate*, a charitable organization, refrained from bringing the ornamented coffer to the house of the painter, in which customarily were laid the deceased's finest clothes or items of a comparable value. There was no reason to bring such a box to Vermeer's home.

A statement by his widow, set down some months after his death: "During the long ruinous war with France [a war that began with the invasion of Louis XIV and his occupation of Guilder and Utrecht] he not only was unable to sell his own art, but even worse the paintings of other artists, on which his business depended, remained on his hands. Because of this and the financial burdens of so many children, and seeing no way out of the situation, he fell into such a frenzy that from one day to another he fell sick and died."

In an inventory taken on February 29, 1676, two and a half months after the death of the painter, it was considered necessary to mention that "in the front room there was a cane with an ivory handle, two easels, three palettes, six panels, two canvases, three volumes of diverse engravings." The materials of Vermeer the painter. The same materials that are used by the painter who has his back turned to us in *The Art of Painting*. A painter who cannot be recognized. A painter of whom we know nothing. Vermeer....

PASCAL BONAFOUX

1

1.
The Rotterdam Gate
was one of the busiest
places in Delft. People
flocked there to meet
ships carrying produce,
to conduct business or
to catch boats going
up and down the river.

At the beginning of the seventeenth century, Delft was the fourth largest city in Holland, with 23,000 inhabitants. (By way of comparison, Amsterdam had 105,000, The Hague 16,000). It was laid out in a classic pattern with streets running perpendicular to each other surrounded by the city walls. This small, peaceful city, built on shady canals, typified the urban character of the Netherlands, compared to the more agrarian cultures of most of its neighbors. Life in Holland was essentially an urban experience, and the Dutch identified strongly with the cities they resided in. In this Vermeer was no exception. It appears that he rarely left Delft, and when he did so, he did not go far. Life in Delft was pleasant. People loitered outside of church or in the town square talking with friends and acquaintances. There were skating parties, lively exchanges in the taverns and most trades were conducted out in the streets. Guild members lived in the same neighborhoods as their fellows. Glass makers could be found on Glassmaker Canal, cheese sellers on Cheese Street and so on. Streets were beginning to be paved, which made it easier to get around by carriage or on foot. Homeowners took pride in their neighborhoods, conscientiously washing down the streets in front of their properties. The Dutch were famous for their cleanliness, though as the canals still served as sewers, conditions were often unhealthy. But compared to the capitals of other European countries, Dutch cities were better tended; the roadways were covered with wooden planks that eased congestion and improved pedestrian traffic.

The Town of Delft

2

2.
Both passengers
and freight traveled
on the Schie to
Haarlem and Leyden.

1. *Rotterdam Gate in Delft*. Jan de Bisschop.
Historisch Museum, Amsterdam.

2. *Boat on the Schie*. Ludolf Bakhuizen.
Historisch Museum, Amsterdam.

3. *Map of Delft, Atlas of Delft*, 1649. J. Blaeu.
Engraving on copper. 37.3 x 48.9 cm.
Gemente Archief, Delft.

4. *Delft Town Hall*, 1667. Dirck van Bleyswyck.
Engraving on copper. 16.7 x 25.6 cm.
Gemente Archief, Delft.

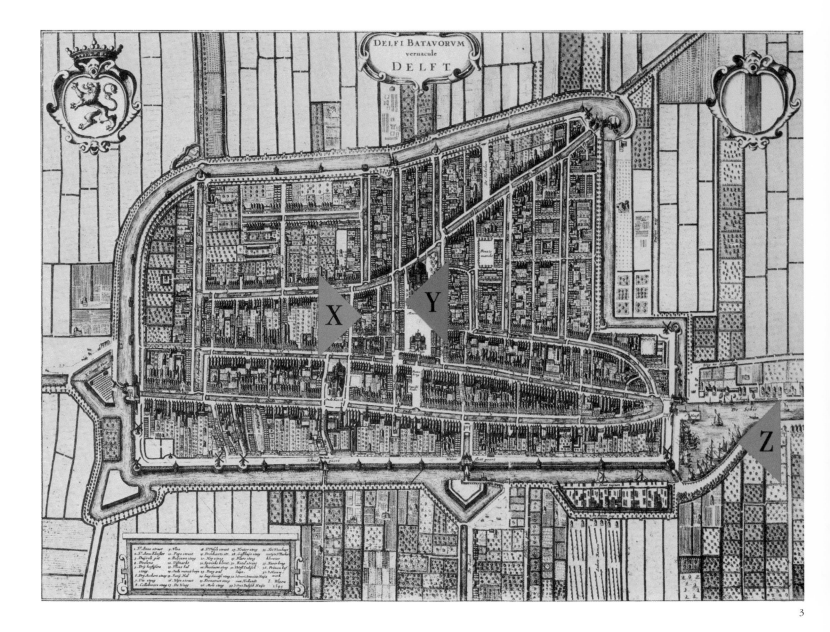

3.
The precision of this map of
Delft makes the identification
of the following sites possible:

X. The Flying Fox, where
Vermeer was born.

Y. The Mechelen, the second
tavern owned by Vermeer's
father.

Z. The spot on the banks
of the Schie where Vermeer
painted his *View of Delft*.

4.

4

Facing each other in
the town square were
the church and the
town hall representing
the two powers that
governed Dutch life.

1.
The Mechelen was the
second tavern owned
by Vermeer's father.
The first was called
Die Vliegende Vos
(the Flying Fox).

1

2.
The Dutch painter Erasmus
Quellinus, a follower of
Rembrandt, received the
important commission of
painting a mural for the
new town hall in Amsterdam.

2

We know more about Vermeer's parents and grandparents than about the painter himself. John Michael Montias spent twelve years sifting through the town archives of Delft and was able to glean much new information concerning Vermeer's family. We now know, for example, that Vermeer's maternal grandfather risked arrest for counterfeiting, and that his paternal grandmother was implicated in a scheme to falsify lottery tickets, after which she worked as a procuress, then became respectable after her third marriage. Vermeer's parents Reynier Jansz. Vos and Digna Baltens were Calvinists. They had a church wedding in Amsterdam in 1615. Soon after they moved to Delft, where they opened a tavern named The Flying Fox (*Die Vliegende Vos*), a pun on Reynier's surname. Reynier was the son of a tailor of a modest background but like some of his more successful ancestors became a master artisan and a guild member. He served as an apprentice in a silk factory in Amsterdam, but in 1631 the register of the Guild of St. Luke refers to him as an art dealer. Vermeer must have been exposed to painting in his father's house. There he would have had the opportunity to meet some of the many artists living in Delft at that time. Reynier and Digna's first child, a girl named Gertruy, was born in 1620. Johannes, the future painter, was born twelve years later. He was baptized in the New Church of Delft on October 31, 1632. This is the only documented indication of his existence until his marriage and admission into the Guild of St. Luke as a master-painter. Both of these events took place in the same year: 1653. He was 21 years old at that time.

3.
Jan Steen, born in 1626,
owned a tavern in Delft
up until 1657. His
popular works often
showed scenes of drunk-
enness and revelry.

3

1. Mechelen Tavern after an engraving by A. Rademaecker, ca. 1710.

2. *Jesus in the House of Martha and Mary.* Erasmus Quellinus.
Oil on canvas. 172 x 243 cm.
Musée des Beaux-Arts, Valenciennes.

3. *Tavern Scene.* Jan Steen.
Oil on canvas. 117 x 161 cm.
Musée du Louvre, Paris. RMN.

4. *Christ in the House of Mary and Martha.*
Oil on canvas. 160 x 142 cm.
National Gallery of Scotland.

4.
Vermeer treats the
biblical story of Christ
with Martha and Mary
in an intimist style.
Steen painted the
same subject in 1653.

4

We know almost nothing about Vermeer's years as an apprentice. The nature of his father's business and the strict rules governing admission into the guilds, do, however, allow some informed speculation as to who his teachers may have been. One name often advanced is that of Leonaert Bramer. Although nothing in their respective styles suggests a deep affiliation, there is documentary evidence that they knew each other. Bramer had acquired a solid reputation in Delft, where after returning from Italy in 1628 he worked in a style influenced by Caravaggio, as did a school of painting based in Utrecht. The fact that Vermeer's early paintings were of biblical and mythological subjects, like much of Bramer's work, seems inconclusive at best, in that not only was this kind of painting very common, but also that Vermeer would abandon it as soon as he became his own master. Another possible candidate is Carel Fabritius. Like Vermeer, he possessed a natural aptitude for light and color. But this brilliant student of Rembrandt was not registered in the Delft Guild of St Luke until 1652. As Vermeer was accepted into the guild in the following year and the required term of apprenticeship was six years, he certainly could not have served his full apprenticeship with Fabritius. A list of other possible teachers overlaps the guild

1
During this era J. van Loo, J. Backer and J. van Noordt distinguished themselves as "history painters." This genre dealt with biblical and mythological subjects.

Apprenticeship

2.
The style of *The Denial of St. Peter* by Leonaert Bramer is derived from the Caravaggists of Utrecht. Instead of daylight, the painter prefers the heightened drama of shadow and candlelight.

2

membership of the time. Two possible candidates are Evert van Aelst and Antony Palamedes. Yet art historians have determined that the clearest influences on the young painter's work came from Amsterdam and Utrecht, from painters such as Erasmus Quellinus. Vermeer's first painting, *Christ in the House of Mary and Martha*, seems to have borrowed some motifs from Quellinus. It would have been easy for the young apprentice to travel down the canals to Amsterdam to admire the large-scale fresco painted by Quellinus for the newly built town hall.

1. *Diana and Her Companions*, 1648. Jacob van Loo.
Oil on canvas. 134 x 167 cm.
Staatliche Museen, Kulturbesitz, Berlin.

2. *The Denial of St. Peter*. Leonaert Bramer.
Oil on canvas. 126 x 141 cm.
Rijksmuseum, Amsterdam.

3. *Diana and Her Companions*.
Oil on canvas. 98.5 x 105 cm.
Mauritshuis, The Hague.

3.
The composition of *Diana and Her Companions* is similar to that of a work by Jacob van Loo. This painting and *Christ in the House of Mary and Martha* were not identified as Vermeers until the 19th century.

3

Painting in Delft

The Guild of St. Luke brought artists together in each major town. The student had to work for six years under the guidance of a member of the guild. After passing an examination at the end of this term the apprentice was elevated to the rank of journeyman. Armed with his diploma, he was free to travel to other cities to find a master who would formally sponsor him for guild membership. Prior to 1650, Delft could not lay claim to a vibrant art scene. Amsterdam, Haarlem, Leyden and Utrecht were considered the leading artistic centers of the day. The more successful of Delft's painters, men like Palamedes and Couwenbergh, were content to excel in somewhat stale and conventional genres. Certainly, Leonaert Bramer, who after his years in Italy could claim a certain originality, and some good painters of still life (Balthasar van der Ast and Pieter Steenwijck) and landscapes (Pieter Grœnewegen) had added luster to Delft's reputation in the 1630. But Delft's real fame coincided with Vermeer's entry into the guild. Unfortunately, existing archives have not shed any light on the relations between Vermeer and the other famous resident of Delft, Pieter de Hooch, who was three years his senior. The two artists, who had to have been friends or rivals, shared a common sensibility, shown in their close attention to interiors, fondness for little streets of red brick and the sweet clarity of their painting. It was at this time that Delft developed a genre all its own, church painting. Notable works in this genre included paintings by Gerrit Houckgeest, Emanuel de Witte and Cornelis de Man. Gerard ter Borch and Jan Steen also honored the city with their presence, although it is not known whether they were acquainted with Vermeer. In 1649, Delft welcomed the eminent landscape painter Adam Pynacker, but the city reached a new level of importance in 1650 with the arrival of Rembrandt's brilliant student, Carel Fabritius.

The Guild of St. Luke was famous for its still-life painters. Balthasar van der Ast first introduced seashells into still lifes. They were brought back from distant lands, and their exoticism seduced painters and Dutch collectors alike.

1

2

2.
From this angle on the Oude Langendijk, where Vermeer lived after his marriage, one can make out the New Church and the town hall. The distortion of the image suggests that this painting was to have been used as an element in a perspective box.

1. *Still Life with Fruits.* Balthasar van der Ast.
Panel. 46 x 64.5 cm.
Mauritshuis, The Hague.

2. *View of Delft,* 1652. Carel Fabritius.
Oil on canvas. 15.4 x 31.6 cm.
National Gallery, London.

3. *Interior of the Old Church of Delft,* ca. 1660. Cornelis de Man.
Oil on canvas. 104 x 123 cm.
Columbus Museum of Art, Columbus, Ohio.

4. *Still Life with Chessboard.* Lubin Baugin.
Oil on canvas. 55 x 73 cm.
Musée du Louvre, Paris. RMN.

3.
Delft could boast of two
beautiful churches and
four artists who specialized
in church painting:
Sarendam, de Man,
Houckgeest and de Witte
loved to represent these
spacious light-filled interiors
or use them as inspiration
for imaginary churches.

3

4.
Contemporaneously in
France, Lubin Baugin
was perfecting the art of
the still life with such works
as *Still Life with Chessboard.*

4

View of Delft

In this painting Vermeer has conjoined an exceptionally fine study of light with a rigorous attention to topographic detail. He is a predecessor in this respect to the succeeding century's Venetian masters, Guardi and Canaletto. In Vermeer's painting the whole city seems to be on display, with its red brick houses, white pointed roofs, high bell tower and bridges covered with trees. Ships are docked along a deserted quay as the sleepy canal flows by the yellow shore, where five or six people are talking. That is the extent of it. "But except for the sky, which is soft and cottony, it is painted with a strength, solidity and firmness of brushstroke rare among Dutch landscape painters." So observed Maxime du Camp in 1859. This tranquility and sweetness with the absence of all movement, this sleeping water that nothing can awaken—the boats are, after all, docked—is certainly the work of a painter who has no taste for scenes of chaos or disorder. In fact, this is the spot where ferries would land, carrying passengers to Rotterdam and The Hague. It was in reality a bustling commercial area, animated and noisy. The extreme precision of each detail and astonishing mastery of perspective tend to support scholars who have theorized that Vermeer made use of an optical apparatus, the *camera obscura*. The principle behind it, already known to Aristotle is as follows: the projection of

"Having seen a View of Delft *in the museum in The Hague, I know that I have now looked upon the most beautiful painting in the world." (Marcel Proust)*

1.

In the 17th century, painters gave over the task of representing cities in a realistic fashion to map makers and geographers. Accordingly the *View of Delft* by Daniel Vosmaer is primarily an imaginary scene. Here the city serves as a pretext for an astonishing study in perspective.

2.
Hendrik Cornelis Vroom was an innovator and meticulous realist. He was, however, occasionally guilty of an oversight: the two ships heading towards each other both have the wind at their backs.

2

light through a small opening into an enclosed dark space creates an upside down image on the interior surface. By projecting this image with the help of a mirror set at an angle one can trace the direct perspective of a scene. Dutch and Flemish painters often used this process, which long before the invention of photography gave their work a rigorous precision. The genius of the painter enters in the subtle blending of the poetic and prosaic in the "profound liquidity and luminescence that Vermeer incorporates in his color." (Elie Laure, 1921)

1. *View of Delft*, 1665. Daniel Vosmaer.
Painting. 90 x 113 cm.
Diemst voor's Rijks Verpreide Kinstvoorwerpen,
The Hague (on loan from the Het Prinsenhof Museum, Delft).

2. *View of Delft, from the North*, ca. 1615.
Hendrik Cornelis Vroom.
Oil on canvas. 71 x 162 cm.
Het Prinsenhof Museum, Delft.

3. (and detail p. 34) *View of Delft*.
Oil on canvas. 98.5 x 117.5 cm.
Mauritshuis, The Hague.

3

Carel Fabritius, beneficiary of Rembrandt's teaching, had moved to Delft at the beginning of the 1650s. Aside from the fact that Vermeer owned three of his paintings, there are no clues to suggest the extent of their acquaintance. Fabritius was only in Delft for four years. In 1654, he met an accidental death due to an explosion of a gunpowder magazine in the house next to the one in which he lived and worked. In seventeenth-century Holland, fire, flood and the plague were ever-present threats to city dwellers. Most houses were constructed from wood, and popular festivals were often celebrated with bonfires that could easily get out of control. In addition, theatrical presentations were illuminated by candlelight. All of these were potential fire hazards. Fires were so frequent that many saw them as an expression of divine justice. Municipal authorities reacted by strictly regulating the hours that furnaces could remain lit. (In Wormer, a town famous for its sea biscuits, a special bell signaled the hours of operation.) Private houses as well as factories kept ladders and buckets in readiness against the possibility of fire. These precautionary measures were insufficient to prevent the explosion that took the life of Fabritius and in the process leveled part of the city of Delft.

In 1667, in his *Description of Delft*, Dirk van Bleyswyck reproduced a poem written by Arnold Bon: "The sad and pathetic death of the most celebrated and talented painter."

Thus was extinguished this Phoenix of our time
In full flight, at the height of his powers
But good fortune rose from the flames that consumed him
Vermeer followed in his footsteps, painter of the hour.

The third edition of Bleyswyck's chronicle slightly modified the original.

Then the Phoenix was cut down in his thirtieth year
In full flight, at the height of his powers
But good fortune arose from the fire that consumed him
Vermeer, a rival equal in stature.

The death of Fabritius, though depriving Holland of one of its finest talents, left the stage free for Vermeer.

1.

To protect themselves from disease, doctors covered themselves from head to foot. The beak of the doctor's mask was filled with perfumes and medicinal herbs.

Vermeer born from the ashes of Fabritius

2.

Jan van der Heyden invented a water pump and greatly reduced the risk of fire by presenting Amsterdam in 1669 with a plan to use oil lamps.

1. *Protective Clothing against the Plague,* 1656.
Engraving. Musée des Arts Decoratifs, Paris

2. *Three Men Using a Fire Hose.* Jan van der Heyden.
Pen and ink. 33.6 x 23.5 cm.
Print Room, Rijksmuseum, Amsterdam.

3. *Portrait of an Old Man.* Carel Fabritius.
Oil on wood. 24 x 20 cm.
Musée du Louvre, Paris. RMN.

4. *Explosion of a Powder Magazine in Delft, October 12, 1654.*
Egbert van der Poel.
Panel. 37 x 62 cm. Rijksmuseum, Amsterdam.

3.
After leaving
Rembrandt's studio,
Fabritius won acclaim
for his daring use of
perspective. Hoobraken
reports that he was
equally adept at portrai-
ture. Despite his short
career, he is considered
to have exerted an
important influence
on Vermeer, de Hooch
and de Witte.

3

4

4.
Shocked by the catastrophe
that cost Fabritius his life,
Egbert van der Poel executed this pictorial account
of the explosion.

Vermeer in *The Procuress* pictures himself raising a glass to the onlooker. His theme, carnal desire, is a well-accepted one in the art of this period as demonstrated in the works of such diverse painters as Couwenbergh, Dirck van Baburen, the school of Caravaggist painters in Utrecht, Terbrugghen, van Ostade and Gerrit Honthorst. In this canvas—the first known to be signed and dated by the artist—the twenty-four-year-old painter has not entirely emerged from the influence of his predecessors. From the Caravaggists, Vermeer borrows dramatic and expressive characterization and an imposing format. From van Baburen, in particular, whose work he must have admired in the home of his mother-in-law, he takes certain poses, such as that of the man in the center of the tableau with his arm thrown around the woman's shoulders. A number of critics and art historians find fault with the composition of this picture. The balustrade over which is slung a tapestry takes up half the painting, while offering a precarious perch for the courtesan's jug of wine. The same tapestry falls to the right with an unlikely fold around the stone balustrade. But despite these awkward details, the painting is audacious and original in two respects: first, in the richness of its characters and second, in the new boldness of its color. Where Vermeer's predecessors illustrated a licentious subject in the smoky light of taverns, emphasizing their dissolute or repugnant features, Vermeer rejects caricature, declines the opportunity afforded for moralizing and does not saddle his figures with leers or grimaces. Rather, they are endowed with personality. Their expressions and gestures are not stereotypical and retain an aura of mystery. One drinks, one looks on, one makes a sexual advance, one blushes. The truth of the canvas is there in its intimacy, hesitations and transgressions. And to this end, Vermeer dares to employ strong contrasting colors against a somber background—the explosive red and yellow of the central figure's garments, the white lace of the woman's hat and collar—which without insolence or prurience illuminate this private scene.

1

1.
Sweerts, a Flemish painter, studied in Amsterdam and Utrecht with the Caravaggists. This painting is distinguished from others on the same theme by its concentration on facial expression and the relationship between the two figures.

2

2.
Vermeer owned Dirck van Baburen's *Procuress*, and he reproduces it in *The Concert* and in *Young Woman Seated at a Virginal*. Close in temperament to the Caravaggists, van Baburen was known for his strong characterization and animated figures.

1. (and detail 1 p. 40) *Young Man and Procuress.*
Michiel Sweerts.
Oil on wood. 19 x 27 cm.
Musée du Louvre, Paris. RMN.

2. (and detail 3 p. 40) *The Procuress*, 1622. Dirck van Baburen
Oil on canvas. 101 x 107 cm.
M. Theresa B. Hopkins Fund.
Museum of Fine Arts, Boston.

3. (and detail 2. p. 40) *The Procuress*, 1656.
Oil on canvas. 143 x 130 cm.
Staatliche Kunstsammlungen, Alte Meister, Dresden.

3

In *The Procuress*, a young gentleman looks out at the viewer with a mocking smile. This is reminiscent of a painting by Couwenbergh, *Scene from a Brothel*, where the painter presents himself to us. Perhaps Vermeer got the idea of a self portrait from Couwenbergh, as René Gimpel, the celebrated art dealer and longtime collector of Vermeer's paintings, had always suspected. Here are some of his arguments for this supposition as proposed in his *Journal of a Collector* (1918-1939): "The young man is posed as one would expect in a self portrait. His shoulder, as when we look at ourselves in a mirror, is too long. He holds his lute in his right hand and his glass in his left; it ought to be the other way around. But it is what one would expect from a picture of a

1

1 to 3.
Other painters, faithful to the iconographic tradition, presented the *Procuress* as toothless and wrinkled.

2

A self portrait?

3

mirror image." Later on Gimpel observes that the head of the figure on the left is not in proportion with that of the courtesan. "It is as if Vermeer did not paint this figure at the same time as the rest of the group. When he placed himself before the mirror, he lost the sense of proportion." In 1929, Gimpel addressed the fact that this model looks older than twenty-four. "It is a well-accepted fact that all young painters, without exception, make their models look older." Just as "a painter with small hands tends to make his models' hands smaller...all his physical shortcomings are reflected in his early paintings. Da Vinci was the first to notice and remark upon this danger."

4.
Vermeer paints a mysterious character of uncertain age. There has been a long debate over whether the figure is a man or a woman.

The marriage of Vermeer

1

Vermeer was Protestant, Catharina Bolnes, Catholic. Religious conflicts crystallizing into a fratricidal war had torn the Low Countries apart in the sixteenth century. The ten southern provinces remained a part of the Spanish empire of the Catholic sovereign Philip IV, while the seven northern provinces declared themselves Calvinist at the union of Utrecht (1579). In 1651, the Great Assembly conferred the status and power of a state religion on the Reformed Church. Catholics were excluded from positions of responsibility and forbidden to practice their religion openly. The authorities were willing to overlook the fact that private houses were being used as churches, but parishioners had to pay generously for this tacit acquiescence. And while there was no open political conflict, social conventions kept relations between members of different faiths to a minimum.

Thus there must have been few opportunities for Vermeer to have made Catharina's acquaintance. He might well have met his future wife at a country fair, during a show presented by one of the numerous troupes of actors that crisscrossed the country or simply in the course of his travels. The Dutch were enthusiastic party-goers: they liked to sing, drink, and eat on river boats; in the winter they gathered for ice-skating on the frozen canals, in the summer for swimming.

After her parents' divorce, Catharina had followed her mother Maria to Delft. Dutch courts looked very severely upon domestic violence. In 1641, Maria Thins scion of a wealthy family of land owners from Gouda, had obtained a separation from her husband, Reynier Bolnes, along with half of his possessions. Despite the possibility of legal recourse, it must have taken all of this independent woman's resolution and determination to free herself from an abusive husband. It is not surprising that Maria had some reservations when her daughter became engaged to be married, on April 5, 1653, to a young painter, who was a Protestant to boot. She did not, however, stand in the way of their union, which was formalized two weeks later in the Catholic village of Schipluy by a Jesuit priest. All of this leads one to believe that Vermeer converted to Catholicism to marry Catharina. Maria welcomed the newlyweds to her house on the Oude Langendijck and helped them financially until her death many years later.

The countryside resembles one large country seat: on the banks of the canals there are trees and hedgerows, many houses, mills for producing lumber and directing the flow of water into the canals.
(Balthasar de Monconys)

2

2.
Churches in Delft were not only used for worship. Children would play in their open spaces, and lovers liked to meet in their private corners, where they could find protection from prying eyes.

3

3.
This painting of frolicking young bathers is unique in the work of Nicolas Maes, a pupil of Rembrandt, who normally painted indoor scenes.

1. *Winter Scene*. Barent Averkamp.
Panel. 40 x 53.5 cm.
Rijksmuseum, Amsterdam.

2. *Tomb of William the Silent in the New Church of Delft*.
Emanuel de Witte.
Oil on canvas. 97 x 85 cm.
Musée des Beaux-Arts, Lille.

3. *The Swimming Party*. Nicolaes Maes.
Oil on canvas. 72 x 91 cm.
Musée du Louvre, Paris. RMN.

Vermeer indifferent to the troubles of his day

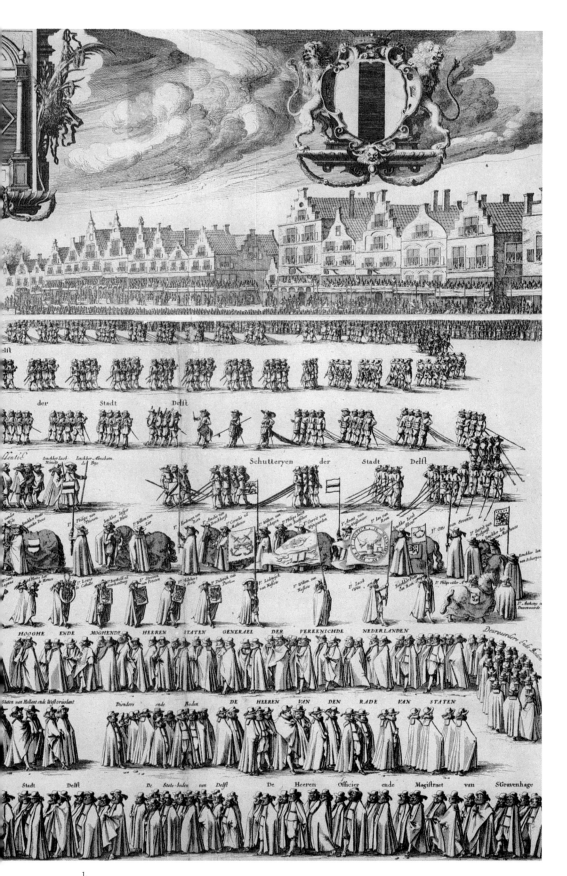

It is astonishing to consider that nothing in Vermeer's painting reflects the troubled world in which he lived. "He lacked a sense of history; human conflicts don't seem to have concerned him," writes A. B. de Vries. As a citizen of the United Provinces, Vermeer was to witness the birth pains of the newly independent republic, the abolition of the Statholderate in 1650 and its reestablishment in 1672. He lived through several wars, the last of which, against France in 1672, ruined his family, and, if one believes his widow, wore him out completely.

In 1632, the year Vermeer was born, the war with Spain had been going on for eleven years. The Twelve Year Peace, concluded in 1609, had resulted only in the cessation of active hostilities. Vermeer was sixteen, when Spain was finally forced to accept the naval superiority of its former colony. It formally recognized the United provinces at the Treaty of Westphalia, signed in 1648. But England, under Cromwell's Protectorate allowed the Dutch little time to savor their victory. The Navigation Act of 1651 prohibited the importation of many types of goods, thereby threatening the Dutch economy, which was entirely dependent on overseas trade. Wars and shifting alliances culminated in the invasion of Holland by the armies of Louis XIV in 1667 and again in 1672. Amsterdam had to open its flood gates as a defensive measure against the invaders. Jan de Witte, the embodiment of the republic, and his brother Cornelis, were blamed for the army's weakness and were both executed. The Stadholderate was reestablished, and the House of Orange once again assumed the reins of power. This was particularly meaningful for Delft, since this royal family had strong connections with the city. All of its princes had been buried there.

Vermeer's work offers a counterweight to the violence of his time. He devoted himself to painting the silence, rootedness and serenity that outside of his interior spaces must have seemed unattainable.

1.
The funeral procession for Prince Maurice in 1625 testified to the power of the House of Orange, whose princes were traditionally buried in Delft. Under the republic, the town was often visited by pilgrims nostalgic for the days of Stadholderate.

1. Fredrick Muller Atlas. *The Funeral Procession of Maurice Prince of Orange-Nassau at Delft, September 16, 1625.* Van Scheyndel. Print Room, Rijksmuseum, Amsterdam.

The Soldier and Laughing Girl

Vermeer painted the *Soldier and Laughing Girl* shortly after the *Procuress*, taking up the theme of sexual love once again.

The relationship between the two figures has often been commented upon. They seem so out of proportion one with the other. In the foreground, the officer seems huge, while the young woman, separated from him only by a corner of a table, is infinitely smaller. This strange perspective can easily be explained as an effect of *camera obscura*, which also can account for the overly brilliant reflection of light on the woman's face, clothes, glass and hands. But we can also discern an intentional distortion

on the part of the artist. The disproportion then comes to symbolically express the relationship between the couple: a delicate young girl dominated by an imposing soldier. The picture's elaborate composition confirms this interpretation. The officer is wedged into a chair the back of which seems prolonged by his belt. His hat is framed by the window frame, the open window and the panel of wood at the bottom of the map. He seems confined within a rigorously delineated space. His fist resting on his leg makes his elbow jut out aggressively into the confined area allotted to his companion. She is circumscribed by the table, the map and the back of her chair. This astute construction imparts to the viewer the undercurrents of tension that the enigmatic expression of the woman—hers is the only face visible—does not communicate. All of Vermeer's seductive power is here. It lies between the visible and the invisible, that which is suggested but never named.

1

1.
This map of the 17 provinces of the Netherlands depicts the naval battles that the country fought with its neighbors at the end of the 17th century.

2.
The East India Company, founded in 1602, continued to prosper. Its vessels traveled to every corner of the globe and returned laden down with the riches of exotic lands. The black sheep of bourgeois families were often sent to man its distant outposts.

2

1. *The Seventeen Provinces of the Netherlands*, 17th century.

2. *Dutch Squadron from the East India Company*. L. Backhuyzen. Oil on canvas. 170 x 286 cm. Musée du Louvre, Paris. RMN.

3. *Market Stall*. Albert Eckhout. Oil on canvas. 106 x 174.5 cm. Rijksmuseum, Amsterdam.

4. *Soldier and Laughing Girl*, ca. 1658. Oil on canvas. 50.5 x 46 cm. The Frick Collection, New York.

3

4

Seventeenth-century Europe witnessed the triumph of the baroque in all forms of artistic expression: in the painting of Tintoretto, in the architecture of Bernini and Borromini, in the music of Monteverdi. The Calvinist ethos of Holland, however, barely tolerated scenes of flirtation that were commonplace in the Italian baroque tradition. For Vermeer, sexual attraction is not expressed by the attitude of his figures, nor by a suggestive decor. In numerous contemporary scenes of this kind, the presence of a

Lady and Gentleman Drinking Wine

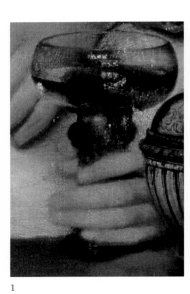 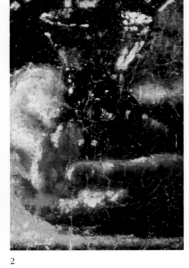  

1   2   3   4

1. 2. 3. 4.
Drinking glasses are present in many of Vermeer's interiors but their significance and treatment change from one canvas to another.

bed, a pair of trousers or of dogs coupling, signals the sexual meaning of the canvas. In this canvas, all of the romantic intrigue is concentrated in a glass of wine. The Berlin painting, in fact, sometimes bears the title, *The Glass of Wine*. Certainly the woman drinks and her suitor stands behind her, holding the flagon of wine ready to refill her glass. But this arrangement does not succeed in negating the woman's reserved pose with her forearm across her stomach, her elbows pressed close to her body and her glance intent on the bottom of the glass. The man's expression is full of sweetness and melancholy. Neither of the figures conveys a suggestion of sexual ardency. Perhaps wine will help them overcome their timidity and in the evening to come the young man will play the lute as the woman sings…. In this work, as in all of his paintings of this period, Vermeer is in the process of developing a style of his own. He applies paint with relatively thick touches, which have a somewhat uneven effect when seen from up close. The vigorous colors and the decisiveness of his brushstrokes are, however, all the more sensitive in that already the painter makes us hear silence and see light.

1. *The Procuress* (detail), 1656.
Oil on canvas. 143 x 130 cm.
Staatliche Kunstsammlungen, Alte Meister, Dresden.

2. *Soldier and Laughing Girl.* (detail), ca. 1658.
Oil on canvas. 50.5 x 46 cm.
The Frick Collection, New York.

3. *Lady with Two Gentlemen* (detail).
Oil on canvas. 78 x 67 cm.
Herzog Anton Ulrich-Museum, Brunswick.

4. *Allegory of the Faith* (detail).
Oil on canvas. 114.3 x 88.9 cm.
Metropolitan Museum of Art, New York.

5. *Lady and Gentleman Drinking Wine* (detail).
Oil on canvas. 65 x 77 cm.
Staatliche Museen zu Berlin, Preussischer Kulturbesitz,
Gemaldegalerie, Berlin.

3

Ever since his marriage Vermeer, had been living with his mother-in-law, Maria Thins. By the end of 1660, his family had grown: Catharina had given birth to three or four children. The eldest, named Maria after her grandmother, was six years old, and the youngest was an infant. Seven years of hard work had failed to make the painter financially self sufficient. On the contrary, despite a regular allowance from Maria, Vermeer had to contract a certain amount of debt. The wills of his mother-in-law (she changed her will at least six times between 1657 and 1680), various

Financial difficulties

1.
Judith Leyster was a pupil of Frans Hals. She illustrated tulip catalogs at a time when three of these bulbs were worth the price of a house. In this painting, it is the woman who is persuading the man to drink.

1

2.
Dutch painters excelled in depicting interiors. The success of this kind of painting depended less on the figures portrayed than on the accessories that surrounded them. Each was rendered with the utmost care and often served as a commentary on the narrative action.

2

formal instruments of debt and the dates of his children who died at a young age constitute the only documentary evidence we have of the Vermeer family from this period. In Maria Thins' first will, the loan of 300 florins made to the couple at their wedding was converted into a gift. Already in April of 1654, Johannes and Catharina had appeared before a notary to guarantee payment of a loan of 250 florins. On November 30, 1657, the couple borrowed an additional 200 florins payable at a rate of 4-1/2% to be repaid in one year to Pieter Claesz. van Ruijven. But if the impressive art collection that he left to his heir Jacob Dissius is any indication, van Ruijven may well have accepted paintings as payment.

The career of the young man was not beginning badly. He was selling his paintings, some of which, unfortunately, have not survived. An inventory compiled in Amsterdam in 1657 includes mention of a *Visit to the Tomb* by "Jan Vermeer of Delft," appraised at 20 florins. Certainly this does not compare to the 300 florins per painting that such artists as Frans van Mieris or Gerard Dou could command, but the price for his paintings was rising with each passing year.

1. *Merry Company.* Judith Leyster.
Oil on wood. 68 x 55 cm.
Musée du Louvre, Paris. RMN.

2. *Cornelis Jansz Meyer, Hydraulic Engineer* (detail). Abraham van der Hecken.
Oil on canvas. 81 x 64 cm.
Rijksmuseum, Amsterdam.

3. *Lady and Gentleman Drinking Wine* (detail).
Oil on canvas. 65 x 77 cm.
Staatliche Museen zu Berlin, Preussischer Kulturbesitz, Gemaldegalerie, Berlin.

1

Lady with Two Gentlemen

2

Vermeer situates this painting in the same room as his *Lady and Gentleman Drinking Wine*. Here is the same tiled floor, the same stained glass window panes. Only the painting on the wall has changed.

The stained glass has been identified. It is the coat of arms belonging to a neighbor of Vermeer, Janetje Vogel. This motif is present in five other paintings by Vermeer. The glass of wine rests at the center of a romantic intrigue. This time it is unequivocal. It is enacted between three people. A couple is united around the glass, and a rejected suitor sulks in the background. There is one unusual aspect of this painting: the young woman directly faces the viewer. She looks out with a malicious gaze. There are certain awkward elements in the composition. The figure in the background seems a bit too far away from the couple although only a table separates them. The young woman's smile seems unappealing, almost a grimace. These factors support the hypothesis that the painting was retouched, probably sometime in the eighteenth century.

3

1. *Lady with Two Gentlemen,* ca. 1662.
Oil on canvas. 78 x 67 cm.
Herzog Anton Ulrich-Museum, Brunswick.

2. *A Lady Drinking.* Pieter de Hooch.
Oil on canvas. 69 x 60 cm.
Musée du Louvre, Paris. RMN

3. *The Card Players.* Pieter de Hooch.
Oil on wood. 67 x 77 cm.
Musée du Louvre, Paris. RMN.

Pieter de Hooch left Delft in 1660, but Vermeer continued to find inspiration in his daring work. With interior scenes, the younger painter had drawn equal to his colleague as much by his meticulous perspectives as by his effects of light. He now set himself a challenge that only de Hooch before him had attempted: the realistic depiction of an exterior scene. *Street in Delft* and the *View of Delft* are the only authenticated open air paintings by Vermeer. A number of others have been attributed to him over the course of time; some of these turned out to be by a Vermeer of Haarlem, another painter entirely who specialized in this genre. Another *View of Delft* in which several houses were represented has disappeared. Thus there remain only these two pictures to testify to Vermeer's excellence in paintings of this kind.

Vermeer "transformed the red brick houses of his country into a daguerrotype animated by spirit." (Edmond and Jules de Goncourt)

Street in Delft

1

1. & 2.
Pieter de Hooch never strayed far from domestic scenes in his choice of subjects. From one side of the threshold to the other, he studied the nuances of interior and exterior light.

2

In Dutch towns of this period, brick was gradually replacing wood as the primary building material. Many facades were washed with lime to prevent erosion and the effects of the salt air. Houses were small, generally no more than two or three stories, although larger ones begin to appear as indications of wealth and status. This canvas, which has known a series of vicissitudes, conveys to us all the serenity of a quiet morning in the year 1660. It was probably sold to Pieter Claesz. van Ruijven and was lost for over a century after the dispersal of the estate of his heir Dissius, in 1682. It reappeared on November 22, 1799, at an auction in Amsterdam.

1. *Back courtyard of a Dutch House.* Pieter de Hooch.
Oil on wood. 60 x 49 cm.
Musée du Louvre, Paris. RMN

2. *Servant and Mistress.* Pieter de Hooch.
Oil on wood.
Hermitage, St. Petersburg.

3. (and detail p. 56-57) *Street in Delft.* ca. 1661.
Oil on canvas. 54.3 x 44 cm.
Rijksmuseum, Amsterdam.

3

The Dutch House

1
Churches, whether real or imaginary, offered Dutch painters, and those from Delft in particular, rich ground for studies in perspective.

W ith the exception of these two cityscapes and some scenes of seduction, Vermeer finds ample room for the expression of his art within the intimacy of the Dutch house, an immobile and silent frame. Pieter de Hooch, Emanuel de Witte and, especially, Samuel van Hoogstraten also used domestic interiors as backdrops for experiments with perspective and light. They broke them down into a thousand fragments that were then reconstituted according to the artist's observations and calculations.

Hoogstraten's box is a dazzling example of the art of perspective. Dutch painters loved to show off their virtuosity. But if they used artificial devices such as magnifying glasses, glass frames and the *camera obscura*, they all looked upon perspective as a means to represent reality as faithfully as possible, not as an end in itself.

The way houses were built lent itself to exercises in style. Direct access to the canals was essential for artisans of every stripe, so the parcels of land bordering the water were as narrow as they were desirable. (They were usually about 7 meters wide.) The height and depth (up to 60 meters) and the way the interior rooms led into one another offered painters the chance to create "a concert of geometry...compositions of squares and rectangles, for which the pretext might be a virginal with its lid up, a half-open window, furniture set at an angle, a ceiling formed by the juncture of three surfaces, the parallel rays of joists or the tiled floor," writes Paul Claudel in *L'Oeil ecouté*.

2.
Looking at this perspective box through a lens, the viewer enters into a three-dimensional representation of a Dutch house.

3

3.
Dollhouses are not only
interesting to children.
Built in the eighteenth
century for a young girl
named Petronella Oortman,
this beautifully constructed
miniature seduced the
painter, Carel Appel.

1. *Ambulatory of the New Church of Delft*, 1651.
Gerard Houckgeest.
Panel. 65.5 x 77.5 cm.
Mauritshuis, The Hague.

2. *Perspective Box.* Samuel van Hoogstraten.
National Gallery, London.

3. *The Doll House of Petronella Oortman.* Carel Appel.
Panel. 87 x 69 cm.
Rijksmuseum, Amsterdam.

After having measured himself against Pieter de Hooch in scenes employing several figures, Vermeer synthesized what he had learned. The result is a canvas that, while small, is perfectly realized.

The painter chose a genre that had fallen somewhat into desuetude: the kitchen painting. Artists such as Pieter Aersten and Joachim Beuckelaer had established a reputation for themselves in the previous century with domestic scenes in which kitchens overflow with food, and the life of the house revolves around the meal that is being prepared.

In Vermeer's painting, there is no agitation. It consists of a single figure who seems so close to us that we feel we could snatch the pitcher out of her hands. A silent and humble activity passes almost unnoticed in this outpouring of materiality: the roughness of the hunks of bread, the fresh liquidity of the milk against the earthenware pot. In the background the wash of lime interspersed with nails and tiny holes focuses our attention on the expanse of gray wall.

Certain critics have interpreted the woman as emblematic of Temperance, who

1.
Daily life as a subject for art made its debut in sixteenth-century engravings. *The Milkmaid* by Lucas of Leyden was one of the first genre scenes.

Maidservant Pouring Milk

2.
Vermeer often used the artifice of a curtain in the foreground to increase the sense of three-dimensionality. But he never came close to approaching the audacious use of trompe-l'oeil that Cornelis Gisbrecht displays in his *Painting Depicting the Back of a Painting*.

pours liquid from one receptacle to another. This trope, however, conventionally calls for water being poured into wine. Rather, it seems that it was the humble and quotidian nature of the activity that attracted the painter. Vermeer seeks to capture the attention of the viewer by sheer technical mastery, and he has achieved an unqualified success.

1. *The Milkmaid*, 1510. Lucas of Leyden.
Engraving.
Print Room. Rijksmuseum, Amsterdam.

2. *Painting Representing the Back of a Painting*.
Cornelis Gisbrecht.
Oil on canvas. 66 x 86.5 cm.
National Museum of Art, Copenhagen.

3. *Maidservant Pouring Milk*, 1660-1661.
Oil on canvas. 45.5 x 41 cm.
Rijksmuseum, Amsterdam.

3

Maidservant Pouring Milk is a good point of reference from which to analyze Vermeer's technique. The lime that covers the back wall seems as real to us as the basket of bread. But Vermeer resorts to two entirely different technical solutions to reconstitute these two different materials. Vermeer's precision even to the smallest detail is often pointed out. With *The Maidservant Pouring Milk,* Vermeer demonstrates his rigorous approach. Observe for example the large empty wall; it asks to be deciphered like a map. Each nail and hole in its textured surface is palpable. The same holds true for the plinth with its squares of faience of which Jean-Louis Vaudoyer observes: "A material so precious, so massive and full that if you were to isolate a small bit of its surface forgetting for the moment the subject matter, you would believe you were

Vermeer's Technique

1

looking at a piece of ceramic, not a painted reproduction." But Vermeer does not treat the chunks of bread and the wicker basket that contains them in the same way. Here it is not possible to identify the object from an isolated fragment. In 1861, the Goncourt brothers raved about "this system of tiny juxtaposed brushstrokes," and "the broad strokes that create a sense of mass." Vermeer's virtuosity can be seen by this alone, his combination of two such disparate techniques in one painting.

1. & 3.
In eighteenth-century Italy, painters such as Guardi used a kind of pointillism in constructing their grand views of the Venice and its canals, a technique Vermeer had already used in *Maidservant Pouring Milk.*

2.
Van Hoogstraten was a brilliant theoretician of perspective and liked to experiment with it in his paintings. After completing his famous perspective box, he turned his attention to trompe-l'oeil.

1. *The Doge in San Nicolo di Lido in Venice, Day of Ascension* (detail). Francesco Guardi.
Oil on canvas. 67 x 101 cm.
Musée du Louvre, Paris. RMN.

2. *Trompe-l'oeil*, 1654. Samuel van Hoogstraten.
Oil on canvas. 90 x 71 cm.
Akademie der bildenen Künste, Vienna.

3. *Maidservant Pouring Milk*, 1660-1661.
Oil on canvas. 45.5 x 41 cm.
Rijksmuseum, Amsterdam.

2

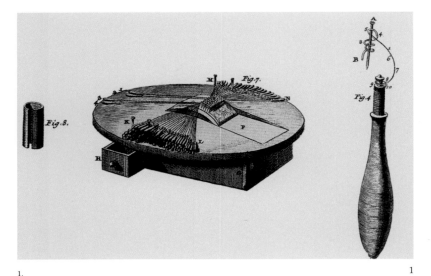

1.
Seventeenth century
engraving of a lace-
making machine.

2.
Netscher's *Lacemaker*
is without a doubt
less virtuous than
Vermeer's. The shoes
and mussel shells
lying on the floor have
sexual connotations.

3.
This embroidered hand-
kerchief is of Belgian
manufacture from the
seventeenth century.

The Lacemaker

With *The Lacemaker*, painted ten years later (ca. 1670), Vermeer attained the complete mastery of the techniques used in *Maidservant Pouring Milk*. In this case, the painter defies the most elementary rules of composition. He subordinates the material to what might seem mere caprice without departing in his choice of subject from an elegant sobriety. For this the smallest of his paintings, Vermeer no doubt made use of the *camera obscura*. Optical effects, such as the blurring of the foreground that brings the figure of the lacemaker into focus, might well pass unnoticed to those familiar with the conventions of photography. But they are not congruent with the way the eye actually sees. If such effects, accented by the oblique angle from which Vermeer chooses to represent the scene, are products of an optical device, the way in which the painter integrates them into the picture is wholly original. The precise rendering of the stretched threads on which the young woman concentrates, contrasts with the audacious blurring of those that fall from the cushion in the foreground. Vermeer drips little dabs of light one by one illuminating the young woman's collar, the ribbon in the yellow book, the tassels on the cushion and the colored motifs of the tapestry covering the table. The discrete vertical composition ensures a rigorous perspective: the center line of the model's blouse leads the viewers' eyes to the work she is concentrating on. In the foreground the pommel surmounting the table leg reinforces the vertical plan.

Without calling attention to itself, Vermeer's complete mastery of his craft allows him to grapple with materiality and subordinate it to his vision of the world. Lawrence Gowring has noted that in this work, Vermeer has gone beyond reproducing palpable phenomena to capture the impalpable world of vision, thereby "transcending logic and reason."

2. *The Lacemaker*, 1664. Caspar Netscher.
Oil on canvas. 33 x 27 cm.
Wallace Collection, London.

4. (and detail pp. 64-65) *The Lacemaker*.
Canvas applied on wood.
Musée du Louvre, Paris. RMN.

4

Young Woman with a Water Jug

Young Woman with a Water Jug takes us once again into the corridors of the Dutch home, in the feminine universe, whose actors are totally absorbed in their daily tasks. Against this backdrop, Vermeer shows us the diverse scenes of daily life. This domestic world was precious to Vermeer; he creates out of it "variations on a symphony of blue, yellow and red." (P.T.A. Swillens)

Just as with the model in *Maidservant Pouring Milk* and *The Lacemaker*, the young woman's abstracted look does not impart her personality. André Malraux suggests that "by the time he was thirty, Vermeer had become bored with anecdote. The sincere sentimentality of his rivals was foreign to him. He knew no atmosphere other than

1

1.
Vermeer faithfully reproduced the best maps of his era. This map by Huyck Allart, does not take into account recent political upheavals. The unfamiliar orientation (north is to the left) was conventional in that period.

2

2.
The care the Dutch lavished on their utensils made the Abbé Sartre remark that "they wouldn't mind dying of hunger as long as they were surrounded by their gleaming pots and pans."

poetry...." It is not his models who create this sense of poetry, but rather the light that sweetens their features, surrounds their hair, permeates their clothing and endows their most mundane activities with a mysterious halo. Here all of the genius of the painter is displayed. His skill in depicting light is such that "a ray that enters from one side of the frame seems to extend to the other side." (William Thoré-Bürger) This powerful technique leads to innovative abstractions, such as that white blob, an audacious rendering of elbow and forearm, which is enough to align the hand that seizes the pitcher with the sleeve of the blouse. It is this perfect balance between the use of light and formal abstraction that reveals the virtuosity of his later work.

1. Map of the Seventeen Provinces, published by Huyck Allart. Private collection.

2. *Silver Pitcher*. Gerard Dou.
Oil on wood. 102 x 82 cm.
Musée du Louvre, Paris. RMN

3. *Young Woman with a Water Jug*, ca. 1662.
Oil on canvas.
Metropolitan Museum of Art, New York.
Henry G. Marquand Bequest.

3

1

*Everything that Vermeer paints
is suffused with memories of
childhood, a calm dreamlike
atmosphere, total stillness and
an elegiac quality too refined
to be considered melancholy.
(Jan Huizinga)*

A Girl Asleep

In *A Girl Asleep*, Vermeer has chosen to
illustrate a classic motif in Dutch painting,
that of drunkenness. The domestic staff of a
Dutch household was not extensive, in contrast to other European countries. Perhaps
because of this, the Dutch servant had
become a kind of institution. Servants were
traditionally engaged on September 29, the
Feast of St. Michael. Lodged in a room off
the kitchen, they had to submit to a strict
regimen but could only be dismissed if they
ran away. The servant became a member of
the family, and it was not rare for her to
spend her entire life in one household.
Often, when she became too old to handle
all of her chores, a younger woman was
hired to help her. She would eat with the
family and served herself before her master,
who had to get up if he needed something,
rather than interrupt her time of relaxation.
Visitors were often not invited back, if they
failed to honor the sacrosanct tradition of
leaving the maidservant a tip.

Vermeer had no interest in acting as historian or sociologist. His servant is
immersed in the calm of this silent room
that acts as a backdrop: a backdrop that is
perfectly constructed, although once again
the painter violates the laws of perspective.
Of note are the diagonal lines from the top
and bottom of the half-open doorway. This
makes the perspective immediately legible.
To suggest depth, the diagonal lines fall
upon the back of the chair with its lions'
heads.

2

1. (and detail 2. p. 73) *A Sleeping Maid and Her Mistress*, 1655.
Nicolaes Maes.
Oil on canvas. 70 x 53.3 cm.
National Gallery, London

2. (and detail 4. p. 73) *Lazy Woman*. Jan Steen.
Oil on Canvas. 38 x 29.8 cm
Hermitage, Leningrad. Scala.

3. (and detail p. 72) *A Girl Asleep*, ca. 1657.
Oil on canvas. 87.6 x 76.5 cm.
Metropolitan Museum of Art, New York.

3

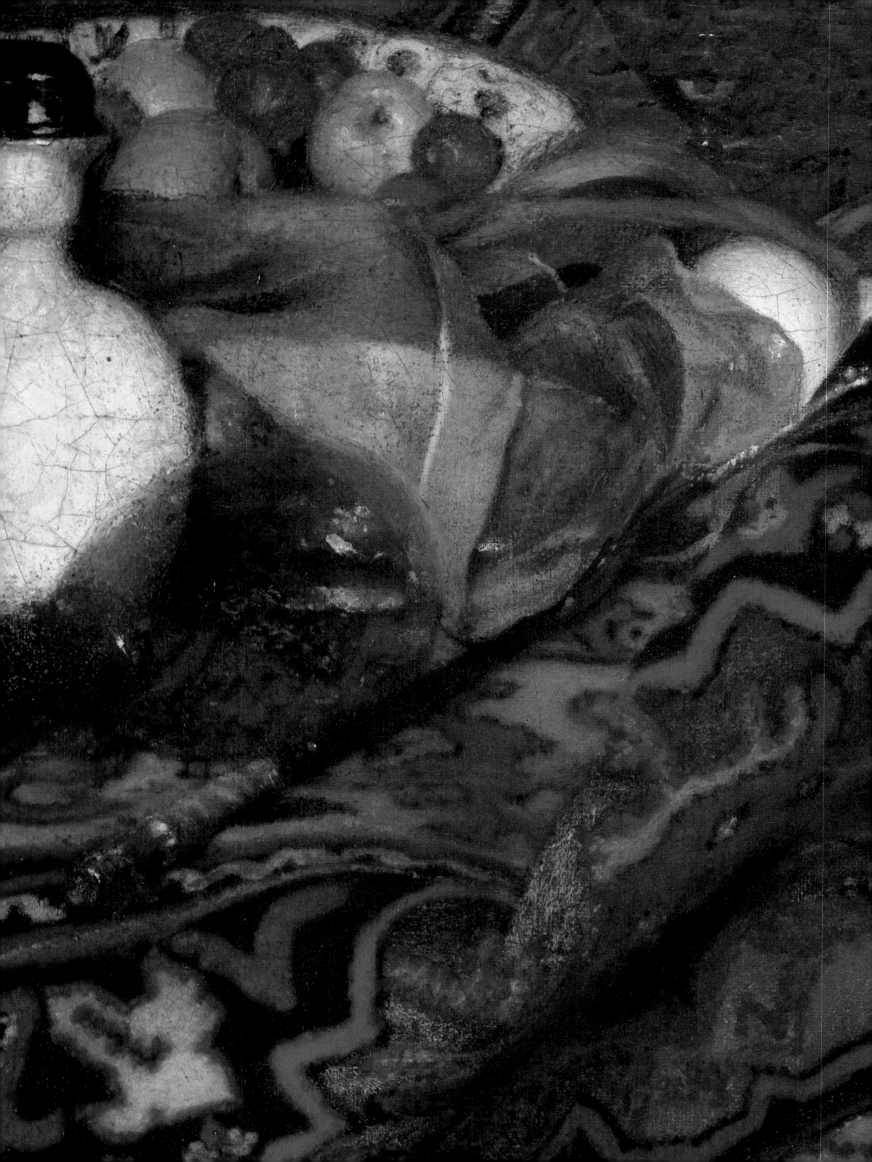

2.
Dirty dishes and the half-eaten remains of a recent dinner are elements traditionally associated with the motif of the idle servant. But Vermeer is never obvious; he makes us look for his moral.

3.
In still lifes, objects have an emblematic significance: the broken glass and watch denote the ephemeral nature of worldly pleasures.

4.
In genre painting each object can be read according to a strict code. One drops one's work and one's slippers to go to bed, either alone or with a companion.

Vermeer invites us to play a game of hide-and-seek. He camouflages and dissimulates where his contemporaries take the opportunity to display their technical skill. The theme of the idle or drunken servant was a popular one. She is represented sitting in front of one or several empty glasses, while around her feet are dirty dishes or laundry. In this painting, only the young girl's rosy cheeks betray her intoxication. The significance of the objects sitting on the table in front of her is ambiguous. The half-emptied glass beside her blends in so well with the table covering that it can easily go unnoticed. Its delicacy and the reflection of her collar in the alcohol are what brings it to our attention. The second glass, although in the foreground, is transparent and lacking precise contours.

Even a second carafe is camouflaged. Lying on its side, it is hidden in the folds of the tablecloth. If we engage in a close examination, we can make out two other objects covered by the tapestry: in the foreground, a knife with a handle of wood or horn, and in the folds of the tapestry, a fork or perhaps a spoon. The riddle of these objects still remains to be solved.

For Vermeer, as we have seen, accessories do not have a simple aesthetic function. They are indices, which, if carefully considered, provide us with keys to the interpretation of the entire work.

3. *Still Life. Breakfast Table*, 1631. Willem Claesz. Heda.
Oil on canvas. 54 x 82 cm.
Staatliche Kunstsammlungen, Alte Meister, Dresden.

Woman with a Pearl Necklace

1

1.
The pious Dutch eschewed
the practice of slavery
on their own soil but felt
no qualms about profiting
from it in their colonial
possessions.

2

The pearl enters the world of Vermeer's painting, never again to leave it. What substance can better capture the subtle nuances of light that this painter so rigorously explores? Its sheen is tempered by the light of the sun; it is satin in the full light of day; luminous at dusk and dawn. In *Woman with a Pearl Necklace*, this dialogue between sun and moon rests on a harmony of yellow and white tones. The young woman who is tying up her necklace in front of a mirror seems subordinate to the painting of the casket of jewels. Her elegance does not easily comport with the Dutch Calvinist ethos. Certain scholars have interpreted the painting as an illustration of the themes of pride, luxury and vanity, often symbolized by the coquetry of a woman applying makeup in front of a mirror. For the historian Jan Huizenga, who was a specialist in the history of seventeenth-century Holland, this casual elegance characterized many of Vermeer's models: "In truth, these women are not part of the aristocracy or bourgeoisie, these creatures clothed in blue, green or yellow jackets, who try on pearl necklaces, receive letters or play instruments. They seem to belong to an unfamiliar demimonde, one that is scarcely acknowledged...." It is this other world born out of the painter's palette that fascinated van Gogh two centuries later. "One can find in these rare canvases all the riches of a complete palette; the arrangement of lemon yellow, pale blue and pearl gray belongs as fully to him [Vermeer] as black, white and gray belong to Velasquez."

PRECEDING PAGES: *Woman with a Pearl Necklace*, 1662-1665 (detail).
Oil on canvas. 55 x 45 cm.
Gemäldegalerie, Berlin-Dahlem.

1. *Young Woman in Front of a Mirror*. Frans van Mieris.
Oil on canvas. 30 x 23 cm.
Staatliche Museen zu Berlin, Preussischer Kulturbesitz,
Gemaldegalerie, Berlin.

7. Polychrome Delft faience, ca. 1700.
Musée des Arts Decoratifs, Paris.

3. Detail from *The Allegory of the Faith*, p. 137.

4. Detail from *The Concert*, p. 99.

5. Detail from the *Love Letter*, p. 121.

6. Detail from *The Letter*, p. 125.

7.
Delft was the center of Dutch ceramic manufacturing. At first influenced by Chinese porcelain of the Ming Dynasty, it developed its own polychrome style toward the end of the 17th century.

8. Detail from *The Messenger*. Jan Verkolje, p. 122.

The Golden Age

1

T he coins lying on the table in *Woman Holding a Balance* are Vermeer's (perhaps unconscious) homage to Dutch prosperity. In Holland more than anywhere else in Europe, the seventeenth century was a golden age. Living in the richest and most densely populated region in Europe, Dutch Calvinists saw

1.
Designed to thwart money clipping, weights and balances were used by money-changers and merchants throughout Europe to verify the value of coins.

2

2. Coins from the United Provinces 18th century.

in their great good fortune God's reward for all the sacrifices they had undergone in His name.

After victory in the war with Spain, free enterprise reigned unchallenged. First, the Dutch transformed their swampy land into a rich agricultural region, and then, this seagoing people set out to seize the riches of distant lands.

The Dutch East India Company, founded in 1602, recorded dividends of 500% to its shareholders in 1650. Amsterdam had become the banking capital of the world. The Exchange Bank, founded in 1609, had gained such trust that its letters of credit, the first debt-based instruments, circulated widely and were considered as reliable as hard money.

Every day speculators gathered in the arcades of the Exchange and pushed share prices higher. The bourgeoisie patronized painters to reflect their commercial success and their strict moral code. Painters' aims naturally coincided with those of their patrons.

3

3.
The United Provinces went to war with Great Britain over the Navigation Act of 1651 that prevented Dutch ships and products from entering British ports.

1. Box of weights from the 17th century.
Musée de la Monnaie, Paris.

2. Coins from the United Provinces, 18th century.
Bibliothèque nationale, Paris.

3. *Seascape with Sailing Ships*, Abraham van de Velde.
Oil on canvas. 35 x 42 cm.
Musée du Louvre, Paris. RMN

4. (and detail on the following page)
Woman Holding a Balance, 1662-1665.
Oil on canvas. 42.5 x 38 cm.
National Gallery of Art (Widener collection), Washington.

4

Woman Holding a Balance

Woman Holding a Balance, which recalls the simplicity of composition of *Woman with a Pearl Necklace*, was appraised for 155 guilders at a public sale in 1696. The auction catalog contains the following description: "A young woman weighing gold out of a box...painted with extraordinary facility and a rigorous manner." *Maidservant Pouring Milk* was the only painting to fetch a higher price.

Here once again are the massive wooden table, the mirror (a little larger here), the standing figure of a woman. The crepuscular light softens the outlines, and the pearls that spill from their coffer catch the last rays of the sun. The motif of the balance, like that of jewelry, points to the vanity of human pursuits. Beauty and wealth are transitory. But Vermeer's painting also lends itself to more complex interpretations. The imposing and solemn picture that hangs in the background, partially obscured by the woman's white cap, represents the Last Judgment. It seems to be by an unknown Dutch painter of the sixteenth century. The art historian Goldscheider theorized that it "could be a later version of a famous work by Jean Bellegambe." Vermeer's painting has also been called *The Weigher of Gold* and *The Weigher of Pearls*, even though the scales are empty. The numerous religious references have convinced the critic Arthur Wheelock that the balance represents the one on which St. Michael weighs the souls of the dead on the Day of the Last Judgment. If, as it seems, the young woman is pregnant, the interpretation becomes even trickier. Vermeer discretely suggests maternity; the two panels of the woman's velvet jacket are slightly puffed out. Its strong color attracts our gaze, but the viewer is left to decide for himself. Is the mother-to-be attempting to discover the future of her child, as Nanette Solomon proposed in 1983?

Here once again time seems suspended. The painting is open to all kinds of interpretations, but neither confirms nor denies any of them.

2

3

2. & 3.
The subject of weighing out gold was treated by Dutch and Flemish painters such as Dou and Rijckaert. Monsters and leering faces in paintings on this subject emphasized the evils of greed and avarice.

2. *The Weigher of Gold.* David III Rijckaert
Oil on wood. 36 x 30 cm.
Musée des Beaux-arts, Lyon.

3. *The Weigher of Gold.* Gerard Dou.
Painting on wood. 38x5 x 22.5 cm.
Musée du Louvre, Paris. RMN

The Astronomer

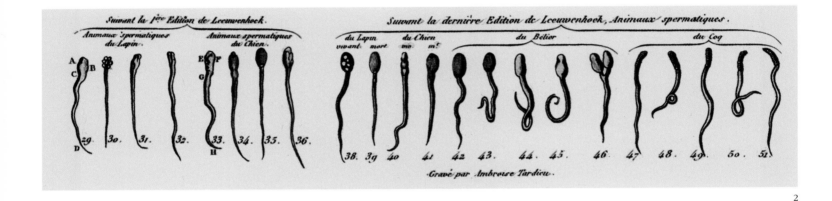

<Along with *The Procuress*, two of the painter's later works, *The Astronomer* and *The Geographer*, are the only ones that are both signed and dated.

In *The Astronomer*, one can make out the painter's monogram on the door of the armoire in the background, along with the date 1668 in Roman numerals.

In a body of work whose inspiration is distinctly feminine, connected to the intimacy and warmth of the hearth, the only two men to whom Vermeer devotes an entire painting are both scholars. In this Golden Age, the astronomer, explorer of the sky, and the geographer, explorer of the seas and distant lands, both fascinated the popular mind. One finds the same concentration in the face of the astronomer as in that of the young woman pouring milk. The same silence and serenity emanates from this well-appointed interior. The table, the tapestry that covers it, the chair and window, all are familiar to us. But here Vermeer applies a new smoother technique. The extreme precision with which he reproduces the book that the astronomer is studying has allowed specialists to establish to a certainty that it is a treatise by Adriaen Metius, *On the Study and Observation of the Stars*, open to the first pages of volume III.

3

1. *Antony van Leeuwenhoek.* Jan Verkolje.
Oil on canvas. 56 x 47.5 cm.
Rijksmuseum, Amsterdam.

2. *Experiments on the Subject of Reproduction.* Antony van Leeuwenhoek.
Engraving.

3. *Philosopher in Meditation.* Rembrandt.
Oil on canvas. 28 x 34 cm
Musée du Louvre, Paris. RMN

4. (and detail on following page) *The Astronomer*, 1668.
Oil on canvas. 51 x 45 cm.
Musée du Louvre, Paris. RMN

3.
Rembrandt was the first painter to portray a sage in contemplation. From the 1630s, his pupils took up this theme, and it became quite popular with this generation of painters and their customers.

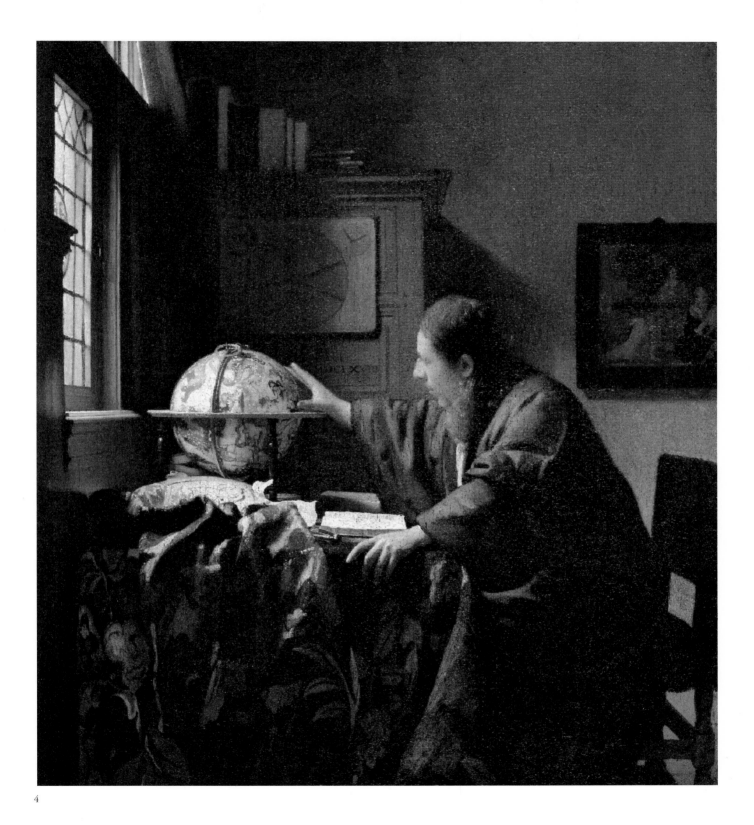

4

The Beginnings of
the Scientific Method

1

On the right hand page of the open book before him the astronomer could read: "The first seekers and investigators of the position and movements of the stars were our ancestors the patriarchs, who, inspired by the Lord God and the science of geometry with the help of mathematical instruments, measured and described for us the firmament and the movements of heavenly

2

bodies." Scientific progress is attributed to divine inspiration as the painting reproduced in the astronomer's study, *Moses Saved from the Waters*, seems to indicate. At the same time, the seventeenth century was witnessing the triumph of rationality. Scarcely had the Copernican theory of heliocentricism been accepted when a stunning new technical development occurred. Metius notes that Galileo and Simon Mayer used the lens, whose properties had been recognized for over fifteen centuries, to observe the stars, thus inventing the telescope. The microscope was another application of the same technology. One of the pioneers in its use was a scientist from Delft, Anthony van Leeuwenhoek, who first revealed spermatozoa to the human eye. He would go from tavern to tavern showing the curious the discoveries of his microscope. The critic Arthur Wheelock has suggested that he is the model for *The Astronomer* and *The Geographer*.

2.
Celestial globes, in the absence of a good working knowledge of astronomy, reflected the persistence of astrology and mythology. The skies were depicted as filled with fabulous animals.

1.
Decorative aspects yielded to the need for precision: scientific instruments became complicated and expensive and were no longer within the reach of the public at large.

3

3.
With his *Geographer*, Braekeleer, a 19th century Dutch painter, revisited a subject that had fallen out of fashion. As one can see, precision was the most important aspect of paintings of this type.

1. *Man Looking Through a Telescope.*
Page from *Discourse in Method* of Descartes, 1637.
Engraving.

2. Celestial Globe. Van Luchtenberg.
Bibliothèque nationale, Paris.

3. *The Geographer* (detail). Henri de Braekeleer.
Oil on wood, 61 x 80 cm.
Musée Royaux de Beaux-Arts, Brussels.

The Geographer

While *The Geographer* clearly carries Vermeer's signature and a date of 1669, no date appears on an engraving after the original executed in 1784. And a watercolor copy done in the eighteenth century by Abraham Delfos shows the date as 1673.

Such contradictions have led some experts to question the authenticity of both this work and *The Astronomer*. It is known that, in five successive sales dating from 1713 to 1797, the two paintings were offered

1.
The Chinese had known that the earth was spherical for over 3,000 years. In classical times, Eudoxius constructed a celestial globe 400 years before the birth of Christ. But in the 16th century, Copernican theorists were still struggling against resistance to the truth of this idea.

1

2

2.
Hugo Grotius, a Dutch jurist and diplomat, was born in Delft, like Vermeer. He was responsible for laying the foundations of international law, which was becoming essential for the growth of trade and colonial empires.

together. It has been recorded that they were offered as pendants despite the fact that both figures are facing in the same direction. Many elements tie the two paintings together: the theme, the figures, the identical dimensions of the two works, the similarity in composition. Most significant is that the celestial globe in *The Astronomer* and terrestrial one in *The Geographer* form a pair of *mappemondes*, identical to that published by Jacob Hondius in 1600.

Since the sixteenth century, terrestrial and celestial globes had become quite popular. The celestial globe could aid in quasi-scientific investigations, while the terrestrial globe, in addition to its decorative function, had many practical applications. One did not have to be a geographer to use the graduated rays that circle the globe to determine with great precision the length of a day at any latitude and at any time of the year. One could also use it to measure the distance between two countries and the sun's position in the sky at a given time and place.

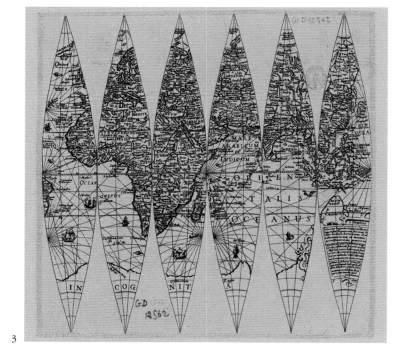

3

3.
Hondius printed flat maps and then pasted them onto globes. This reduced production time and costs and permitted their widespread distribution.

1. Chinese Mappemonde, 1674. Nan-Hoei-Saïn. Bibliothèque nationale, Paris.

2. *Hugo Grotius.*
Engraving
Bibliothèque nationale, Paris.

3. Terrestrial Globe in Zones, 1615. Jacob Hondius. Bibliothèque nationale, Paris.

4. (and details 5, 6 & 7, p. 88) *The Geographer*, 1669. Oil on canvas. 53 x 46.6 cm. Stadelsches Kuntinstitut, Frankfurt.

4

2.

This mathematician is caught in the process demonstrating a formula. The austerity of his demeanor is characteristic of the Dutch Calvinist.

1.

Adriaen van Ostade, a pupil of Frans Hals, was known for his humble and often grotesque subjects. In works such as this painting of a scholar, he succeeds in instilling life and color into conventional themes.

1

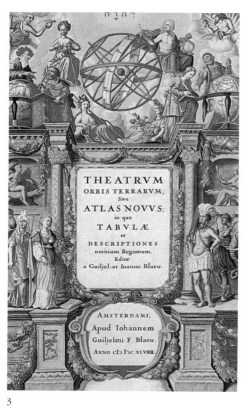

3

3.

One of the most famous cartographers, Jan Willem Blaeu, devoted his entire career to making the recent discoveries of the far regions of the world known to the general public.

2

4.

Johann Schöner, like most scientists of this period, was a churchman. On this globe, constructed in 1520, he confirmed the separation between the Asian and American land masses two centuries before the fact was widely recognized.

1. *Chemist in His Laboratory* (detail). Adriaen van Ostade.
Oil on wood. 28 x 22 cm.
Staatliche Museen, Kulturbesitz, Berlin.

2. *Portrait of a Mathematician.* Ferdinand Bol.
Oil on canvas. 77 x 63 cm.
Musée du Louvre, Paris. RMN.

3. Frontispiece from *New Atlas.* Jan Willem Blaeu.
Published in Amsterdam, 1649.

4. Terrestrial globe on painted wood, 1520. Johann Schöner.
Germanisches Museum, Nuremberg.

5

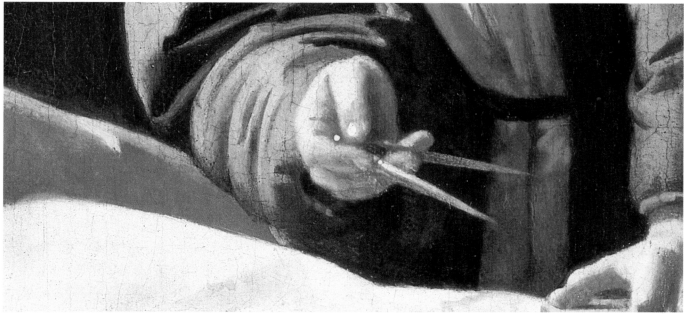

6

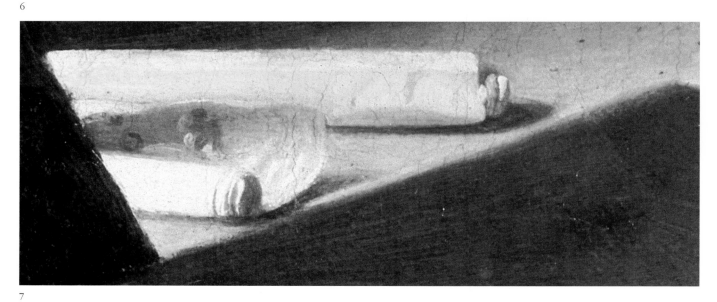

7

The Guitar Player

On October 18, 1662, Saint Luke's Day, the burgomasters of Delft elected the syndics for the three corporations of the city's guild: that of the faience makers, the glass makers and the painters and sculptors. At thirty years old, Vermeer became the youngest syndic of the guild since its reorganization in 1613. With his election and with the recent departures of Pieter de Hooch and Emanuel de Witte, he became a prominent figure in the artistic life of the city.

When Balthasar de Monconys, an advisor to the French court, accompanied the young Duke de Chevreuse on his European tour during the summer of 1663, it was natural for them to stop in Delft to pay a call on Vermeer. Unfortunately, the painter was unable to show them any finished paintings. In the journal he kept of his travels, Monconys records: "We saw a painting at a baker, who was said to have paid 600 livres for it, although there was only one figure in it. I don't think it was worth 6 pistoles." Monconys' evaluation seems to rely more on the format and the number of people portrayed than on the intrinsic quality of the

1

2

painting. This brings to mind an anecdote recounted by Jean Mistler of the French Academy, about one of his friends, an admirer of Rembrandt, who remarked: " You're not going to compare your Vermeer to Rembrandt. Thirty of his paintings cover no more than 30 square meters, while *The Night Watch* alone measured almost 20 before it was cut."

1. & 2.
The type of short satin or velvet mantel bordered in ermine that is seen in Metsu's painting, and in many other genre scenes as well, is similar to the one Vermeer often dressed his models in. During this period, ermine was also considered a prerogative of royalty, as shown in this imposing portrait of Louis XIV by Hyacinthe Rigaud.

1. *Portrait of Louis XIV in Royal Costume*, 1701.
Hyacinthe Rigaud.
Oil on canvas. 277 x 194 cm.
Musée du Louvre, Paris. RMN.

2. *Woman Reading a Letter*. Gabriel Metsu.
Oil on wood. 52.5 x 40.2 cm.
National Gallery of Ireland, Beit Collection, Dublin.

3. *The Guitar Player*, ca. 1661.
Oil on canvas. 53 x 46.3 cm.
The Iveagh Bequest, Kenwood, English Heritage.

3

The Lutenist

1

1.
Ter Borch traveled to
Italy and Spain. He was
influenced by the baroque
style, but at the same time
one sees elements used
in Dutch genre painting,
such as the short mantle
and the tapestry covering
the table. Ter Borch was
particularly skilled at rendering clothing and fabrics.

*In an interior with furnishings, a seated woman in costume
plays the guitar. Striking use of light, fine execution on wood.
(Auction catalog from Amsterdam, December 22, 1817)*

*T*he *Guitar Player* and *The Lutenist* are
the only two paintings in which Vermeer represents a musical theme with his figures
painted seated in the style of the Italian quat-
trocento. Both figures are alone, and the
music seems to lend support to their reveries.
But their luminous glances betray an
amorous impatience. Music and romance
have always complemented each other. In
Italy of the sixteenth century, the depiction of
music in painting was still restricted to biblical and mythological scenes, such as Titian's
Venus and a Lute Player.

In the following century, the music parties that are so often seen in the paintings of
Caravaggio and his followers, immediately
became popular with Dutch painters based in
Utrecht. The characters in these dramas do
not come from the pages of mythology but
rather from the demi-monde of the tavern. In
these night revelries, entertainers wearing
make-up strike outlandish poses, drunk even
before they begin singing for their clientele,
as in van Baburen's *Procuress.* It required the
delicate sensibility of van Mieris and Vermeer
to bring music into the sanctum of the Dutch
home. There it accompanied a hesitant
amorousness, one that often was too timid to
declare itself.

2

1. *A Woman Playing a Theorbo to Two Men*, ca. 1668.
Gerard ter Borch.
Oil on canvas. 67.6 x 57.8 cm.
National Gallery, London.

2. *The Duet.* Hendrick Terbrugghen.
Oil on canvas. 106 x 82 cm.
Musée du Louvre, Paris. RMN.

3. *The Lutenist*, ca. 1664.
Oil on canvas. 51.4 x 45.7 cm.
Metropolitan Museum of Art, New York,
Bequest of Collis P. Huntington, 1900.

2.
Terbrugghen encountered
the work of Caravaggio in
Rome, and it made a deep
impression on him. This
painting uses Caravaggist
elements—the large scale
of the canvas, the strong
composition, the use of
light and shadow—in rendering a typical genre scene:
the musical duet.

3

1

The Music Lesson

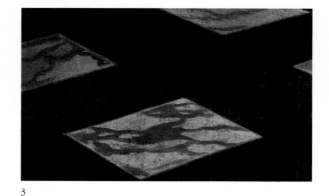

1.
The piece of wood furniture
reflected in the mirror in
The Music Lesson is not
shown in the painting
itself. Is this out of a
concern for realism, or is
the painter sharing a joke
with the spectator?

2. & 3.
The reflection in the
mirror of these two details
shows with what care their
proportions were handled.

2

3

Analysis of *The Music Lesson* is quite
"straightforward" according to Edgar A.
Snow: "The human element has been pushed
into the margins of the painting, beyond the
viewers capacity to appropriate it. But this
results in a new kind of intimacy. We feel that
we can approach more closely that from
which we are normally excluded by the overly familiar proximity of scenes of this kind."
This is a rather subtle contradiction: the sen-
sation of intimacy arises from the very distance that Vermeer places between his figures
and the viewer. On a flat surface the painter
has created an uncanny sense of depth,
thanks to his rigorously controlled composition. Horizontal, vertical and diagonal lines
are balanced one with another. The image
that the mirror offers us allows us to precisely gauge the distance separating us from the
back wall. Claudel enthused over such "com-
positions of squares and rectangles for which
the pretext [is] an open virginal…." The per-
sonalities and emotions of the actors in this
tableau pass almost unnoticed. Only the
pitcher on the table and the motto inscribed
on the open case of the virginal, *musica
laetitiae comes medicina dolorum* (music is a
companion in joy and a comfort in sorrow),
suggest that perhaps what we have before us
may not be a simple music lesson.

4. (and details 1, 2 & 3) *The Music Lesson*, ca. 1664.
Oil on canvas. 73.3 x 64.5 cm.
Royal Collection, St. James Palace,
Her Majesty Queen Elizabeth II.

4

The Concert

1

1.
Alessandro Scarlatti (1660-1725) was musical director for the Court of Naples and one of the fathers of Italian opera. He left behind a diverse body of work that includes cantatas, oratorios and keyboard pieces.

Musical instruction was not only meant to complete the education of the Dutch bourgeoisie; it was a common fact of life throughout this period. The reform church had succeeded in stamping out public concerts, but against musical evenings held in private homes it was altogether powerless. The composition in *The Concert* and *The Music Lesson* is similar. In both paintings, the rectangular picture frames and tiles play off one another. Charles de Tolnay observes: "Vermeer likes to place very large objects in the foregrounds of his paintings. They serve to push objects in the middle distance and the background farther away." This trio is, however, closer to the viewer than the figures in *The Music Lesson*. The cavalier who has his back turned is playing the lute. On his right one woman sings, on his left another plays the virginal. There is nothing here to distract them from their music. At least one might suppose so. But the paintings hanging on the wall behind them lend another interpretation to this scene, where all emotions seem kept out of sight. Once again, Vermeer offers us only indications.

2

2.
Claudio Monteverdi (1567-1643) was the musical director of St. Mark's in Venice. Though famous for his liturgical music, he also composed some of the most beautiful operas of the baroque period: *Orfeo*, *The Coronation of Poppea*, and *The Return of Ulysses*.

3

3.
Like many of his Dutch counterparts, the French painter and engraver Claude Vignon made the obligatory trip to Rome. Like them, he was strongly taken by Caravaggio, although his work betrays a strong mannerist influence.

---

1. *Alessandro Scarlatti*. Engraving.

2. *Claudio Monteverdi*. Engraving.

3. *The Young Singer*. Claude Vignon. Oil on canvas. 95 x 90 cm. Musée du Louvre, Paris. RMN.

4. (and detail on preceding pages) *The Concert*. Oil on canvas. 72.5 x 64.7 cm. Isabella Stewart Gardner Museum, Boston.

The spectator is free to choose an interpretation that suits him. The scholar and art critic Pomme de Mirimonde has suggested the following scenario. The singer, who is older than the two musicians, is cast in the role, perhaps unwillingly, of the procuress in the Baburen painting hanging behind her. In the same vein the landscape on the wall in the style of Ruysdael, hints at the instability of love, and the couple can expect to be exposed to the full brunt of its storm.

4

Young Woman Standing at a Virginal

Dressed in a fine gown, looking calmly at the spectator with a slightly ironic smile, the young woman in this painting remains mysterious and enigmatic. The Cupid behind her, a picture within a picture, has the charge of carrying the message of love.

This canvas, which was once attributed to Cesar van Everdingen, has not met with universal approval. Some critics have looked for extenuating circumstances. "One suspects that Vermeer had to paint this work either to please the lady herself or her husband," writes M. Lucas.

2 Street singers.

André Chastel speculates about the painting of Cupid: "...it is exactly proportional to the painting of which it forms a part. This tableau, which figures so prominently, tends to assume a heightened importance, as if it furnished the psychological key to the entire canvas."

Pomme de Mirimonde preferred to confine himself to an analysis of the musical elements in the painting. He notes that its erstwhile title, *Young Woman in Front of a Spinet*, was given to the work some time after the Vermeer's death, possibly as late as the nineteenth century. He goes on to observe that this is somewhat inaccurate, since the instrument in the painting is not a spinet, which is without legs and rests on a table, but rather a virginal, an instrument that had recently been imported from England.

The preoccupations of scholars, no matter how intensely argued, do not, however, prevent us from basking in the charm and serenity of this lovely work.

1

1.
Frans van Mieris was a student of Gerard Dou. He specialized in painting interior scenes. In the *Duet* those familiar with his painting will recognize certain elements: the chair, the use of a curtain as an element of trompe l'oeil, the painting within a painting. But here the painter subordinates decorative elements to the scene which is being acted out.

3

3.
Sheet music of this period from Holland is practically impossible to find. A strict Calvinist outlook kept musical performance within the confines of the family. Dutch music of this period seems rudimentary compared to the grand achievements of the Baroque.

1. *Duet*, 1658. Frans van Mieris.
Oil on canvas. 31.5 x 24.6 cm.
Staatliches Museum, Schwerin.

2. *Street Singers*, 17th or 18th century.
Engraving.
Bibliothèque nationale, Paris.

3. Page from the musical score of *Bellérophon*
(opera by Lully).
Printed in Paris in 1679.
Christophe Ballard.

4. *Young Woman Standing at a Virginal*.
Oil on canvas. 51.7 x 45.2 cm.
National Gallery of Art, Washington.

4

Young Woman Seated at a Virginal

1

1.
Musical instruments typically found their way into Dutch genre paintings. In other European countries, painters such as Evaristo Baschenis incorporated them into still lifes.

In this painting as in the preceding one, the original title names a spinet rather than a virginal. The confusion may be explained by the fact that the titles of many of the thirty-five works that are today attributed to Vermeer were given to them by the art lovers of the nineteenth century who "discovered" them.

Keyboard instruments became extremely popular in the Lowlands as soon as they were introduced, in part because they were easier to play than stringed instruments such as the lute or theorbo. The viola da gamba, whose sweet sonority blended harmoniously with the clavier, was also highly prized. Vermeer includes it in *The Music Lesson.* Other popular stringed instruments were the guitar, already well-known in Spain and Italy and the mandola, ancestor of the modern mandolin.

The Dutch were music lovers. Each of the corporations of which the guilds were composed had its own repertoire of songs. The weaver, the coach maker, the servant, the lover, all had songs of their own to express the joys and sorrows of life. A marriage ceremony was not complete without a concert, even though there were strict rules governing the number of instruments that could be played. All despite the fact that liturgical vocal music was the only kind of music officially recognized. In 1640, the organ was reintroduced into religious services. As it helped fill the churches, the preachers allowed it to stay. It is on account of this relaxation of the strict Calvinist practice that at least one Dutch name can be inscribed in the history of music of the seventeenth century: Swelinck, the organist of the Old Church in Amsterdam.

2

2.
Painters' fascination with musical instruments did not die out with the Baroque. In the 20th century the founders of cubism, Picasso and Braque, used string instruments in their geometric deconstruction of space.

1. *Musical Instruments.* Evaristo Baschenis.
Oil on canvas. 98.5 x 146 cm.
Musée Royale des Beaux-Arts, Brussels.

2. *Violin*, 1912. Pablo Picasso.
Papier collé.
Pushkin Museum, Moscow.

3. (and detail p. 105) *Young Woman Seated at a Virginal,*
ca. 1674.
Oil on canvas. 51.5 x 45.5 cm.
National Gallery, London.

3

While Calvinism was attempting to keep music in the Netherlands within the confines of the liturgy, the rest of Europe was enjoying the splendor of the Baroque. Gabrielli, Monteverdi and Schutz were inventing a new style in which voice and instruments joined together in harmonious conversation. The concerto form underwent a process of continual development from Vivaldi to Bach. Handel showed himself a master of opera, in which Scarlatti also excelled, as well as oratorio. Even in the studiously classical France of Louis XIV, the court ballets and operas of the Florentine composer Lully were warmly received. All of these diverse musical forms

A Calvinist Enclave in the Age of the Baroque

1

1. & 2.
In 1947, Jackson Pollock inaugurated the technique of "dripping" which consisted in using the whole body to throw paint or other elements onto the canvas. The interlacing of lines obtained in this way in *Number 19* recalls the marble in the trompe l'oeil painted by Vermeer in *Young Woman Seated at a Virginal*.

were born in this one century, which can also claim to be the age of reason.

The music played in Dutch homes was built around a text. Each emotion was codified and conventionalized; each passion corresponded to a particular harmony. As theater and dance were not nearly as well accepted by ecclesiastical authorities, municipalities often had to forego their enjoyment of these forms to placate the church. Politics and theology were closely intertwined. In 1668, the acting troupe of the Queen of France requested permission from the Prince of Orange to produce a theatrical piece in The Hague. The church immediately sent an envoy to William III, resulting in his imposing certain restrictions: no scandalous subjects and no performances on days when the Gospel was being preached.

1. *Number 19*, 1949. Jackson Pollock.
78.7 x 57.7 cm.
Private collection. By kind permission of Galerie Gerald Piltzer, Paris.

Girl Interrupted at Her Music

Many elements in this painting will appear familiar to us: the chair with the lions' heads, the stained glass motif in the window, the famous painting of the Cupid. The chair placed next to the window and the way the light falls on its back might also bring to mind another painting: the *Lady and Gentleman Drinking Wine*. And yet many art historians have questioned the authenticity of the *Girl Interrupted at Her Music*. From 1810, date of its first authenticated sale, until its purchase in 1901 by the prominent American collector, Henry Clay Frick, its descriptions in catalogs have differed a little more than more than one would normally expect. In the catalog of 1811, a birdcage and a violin with a bow are mentioned. In 1899, Hofstede de Groot remarked on a fragment of a fireplace on the right and noted the effects of an "energetic cleaning." Today, the painting is not in sufficiently good condition to be subjected to a thorough examination. Nonetheless its undeniable pictorial quality and the sweetness of the treatment and the models' expressions, which immediately engage the viewer, have convinced most critics that the painting could be by no other hand than Vermeer's.

1

1.
Music director for the court of Louis XIV, the Florentine Lully while defending the French classical tradition, introduced elements from the Italian Baroque, which was becoming the dominant musical style throughout Europe.

2

2.
The New Theater of Amsterdam was built in 1637 at a cost of 20,000 florins. Even though a large part of its revenues were allocated to public charities, it ran afoul of religious authorities. They objected to such frivolous entertainments and harshly criticized the building itself, maintaining that the boxes on the upper floor were designed for flirtation and licentious behavior.

3.
Lully like his patron Louis XIV was an absolute monarch in his field. He monopolized the opera with his own works, drove Molière's troupe of actors out of the Palais-Royal and founded his own academy of music.

3

1. *Performance of* Thetio, *a Ballet by Lully, in the Petit Bourbon Theater*, 1654.
Engraving by Crépy after Aveline.

2. *Interior of the New Theater in Amsterdam*, S. Savery.
Engraving.
Print Room, Rijksmuseum, Amsterdam.

3. *Jean-Baptiste Lully*. Engraving.

4. *Girl Interrupted at Her Music.*
Oil on canvas. 39.3 x 44.4 cm.
The Frick Collection, New York.

4

Europe's Finest Postal System

1

To compensate for the poverty of their soil, the Dutch turned to industrial development. In the seventeenth century, Holland's economy, on account of its manufacture of textiles, paper and porcelain, was thriving. This commercial orientation called for the establishment of efficient communication and distribution networks. On land and sea, the Dutch transportation system was the best of its time. The nascent postal system benefited from these advances and in turn spurred them on. Letters were sent by post from Amsterdam before the end of the seventeenth century.

Just as in England, education was a priority for the Dutch Reform Church. At the end of the century, the citizens of these rival powers were the best educated in Europe. All rungs of the social ladder benefited from this emphasis on learning, which was spearheaded by the preachers and school teachers. In a short period of time, the Dutch postal system found itself catering to a highly literate population that took enthusiastically to the art of correspondence. Epistolary manuals provided stock forms, offering the uninspired lover a range of possibilities, all in elegant and demure turns of phrase. The most popular of these was a French work by Jean Puget de la Serre, *Le Secretaire à la Mode*, which went through numerous editions after its first publication in Dutch in 1643.

2. Detail from *The Love Letter*, p. 121.

2

1. & 3. Early letters with postage stamps.

1. & 3.
The first Dutch postage
stamps were used for
service linking Amsterdam
and Rotterdam. This
was the beginning of
regulating postal rates.

3

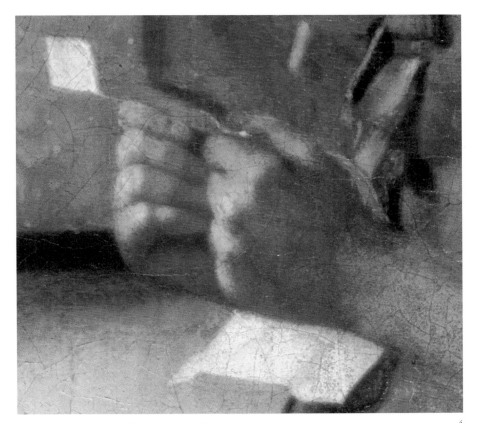

4. Detail from *Woman Reading a Letter*, p. 115.

4

Writers and Philosophers

Posterity has paid considerably more attention to the love letters depicted by Dutch painters than the work of their fellow writers and poets. No doubt this is in part because the language of painting is universal, while writers are limited by the reach of their native tongue. Nonetheless, a Dutch literary tradition does exist, even if its status remains somewhat undefined. Paradoxically, while the country offered asylum to philosophers whose thought they found subversive (Descartes, Spinoza), it recruited its authors from the establishment. Figures such as Pieter Cornelisz. Hooft (1581-1647), the son of a burgomaster, and Constantin Huyghens (1596-1687), secretary of the Stadholder, were cultivated individuals, immersed in the

1.
Spinoza was born in 1632, the same year as Vermeer. He came from a marrano family, Spanish Jews forcibly converted to Catholicism by the Inquisition. He obtained political asylum in Amsterdam where he was able to devote himself to philosophical studies in a climate of tolerance.

BENOIT SPINOSA
Né à Amsterdam, l'An 1632 Mort le
21. Fevrier 1677. Âgé de 44 ans.

1

2

masterpieces of the Italian renaissance or seduced by the excesses of mannerism. They tried their hands at poetry, satire, history and tragedy. The force and acuity of his satirical writings earned Joost van Vondel (1587-1679) the title, "the prince of poets," even though he was a convert to Catholicism. The popularity of Jacob Cats (1577-1660) was unmatched: only the Bible sold more copies than his work. Known as "Father Cats," he was the incarnation of Calvinism. He wrote on themes from daily life, without pretension or humor. Does this mean that painting somehow sidestepped the didactic and moralizing spirit of the time? Not altogether. Pictorial symbolism was placed in the service of edifying principles. But today we can enjoy its artistic qualities and leave the message behind.

2.
Descartes took up residence in Holland in 1629 and remained there for 20 years. Like Rembrandt, he took a servant, whom he had met in a tavern, as his common-law wife. They had one child, who was never legitimized by the ecclesiastical authorities.

3

1. *Baruch Spinoza.* Engraving.

2. *Descartes.* After Frans Hals. Oil on canvas. 77.5 x 68.5 cm. Musée du Louvre, Paris. RMN.

3. *Blaise Pacal.* Edelinck. Engraving.

4. *Woman Reading a Letter.* Oil on canvas. Staatliche Kunstsammlungen, Alte Meister, Dresden.

3.
Mathematician, physician and philosopher, Blaise Pascal remained in France finding there a Jansenist austerity compatible with his temperament. The walls of the Palais-Royal, within which he retired, formed a bulwark against Jesuit decadence.

4

Woman Reading a Letter

1

1.
In this painting by
Pieter de Hooch, a
mother removes lice
from the head of her
child. With the discovery
of the microscope lice
became a frequent subject
of scientific investigation.

The letter, just as the musical instrument, served as a vector for amorous discourse. The act of writing or receiving a letter afforded painters the opportunity to surprise the young daughters of the bourgeoisie in the midst of their romantic reveries. Gerard ter Borch, Gabriel Metsu and Jan Steen all were masters of the depiction of this essentially feminine theme. Six of Vermeer's paintings feature letters.

All of these young women are shown dressed very elegantly, in their own homes, usually attended by a servant. The time that they seem to have for matters of the heart is undoubtedly a privilege of their elevated social standing. Most Dutch women had little time to devote to love. Their families assumed the responsibility to find them good husbands, and the relations between courting couples were quite strictly codified, sparing them the need for any initiative in romantic intrigue. Infatuation and the intoxications of romantic love were frowned upon in this bourgeois society. The most highly esteemed women were those whose tastes were simple and manner unassuming. Once married, they were to handle all domestic duties and assume the responsibility for raising and educating children, thus allowing their husbands to devote themselves wholeheartedly to their ruling passion, the conduct of business.

Erotic subjects, far from being taboo, were quite liberally broached in daily conversation, as much by women as by men. The rest of Europe blushed at the frank speech of their Dutch neighbors.

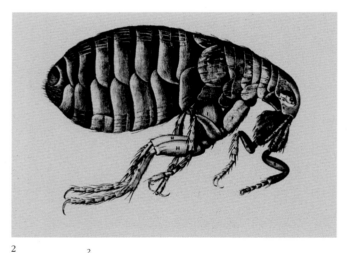

2

2.
The English mathematician
and astronomer Robert
Hook had been studying
natural sciences for only
two years when he executed
this meticulous rendering
of a flea.

1. *A Mother's Duty*, Pieter de Hooch.
Oil on canvas. 52.5 x 61 cm.
Rijksmuseum, Amsterdam.

2. Flea seen under a microscope from *Micrographia*, 1665.
Robert Hooke.

The two *Readers* of Vermeer deal with the same subject but in completely different ways. The Dresden *Young Woman Reading a Letter* (page 111) is undated, but experts consider it to be an early work, painted circa 1659. X-rays have revealed Vermeer's hesitancy in his execution of the painting. The young woman seems initially to have been standing farther to the left and facing in a different direction. The Cupid, attributed to Everdingen, originally hung on the back wall. The red curtain seems to have been a late

Maternal Silence

1

1. & 2.
The work of Vermeer, unlike that of some of his colleagues, is marked by the utmost delicacy with which he handled the theme of maternity. Scientific researchers struggled for a long time against the taboos concerning sexuality and reproduction. If da Vinci had published his notebooks, science would have been advanced at least one hundred years.

addition. Despite these reworkings, *Young Woman Reading a Letter* stands out as one of the painter's most technically accomplished renderings. The curtain, the red tapestry, the reflection of the woman's face in the window, the letter, which is crumpled from being read and reread, all contribute to an almost theatrical presentation of an immobile and silent exaltation. The stillness and silence that characterizes the atmosphere of the Amsterdam *Young Woman Reading* is of an entirely different order. Diffuse lighting and harmonious blue tonalities bathe this tapestry of ripening maternity with an absolute serenity. This canvas is as small as the other is large. Here one has to look carefully to make out the letter, which blends in with the neutral tones of the background. In the Dresden painting, the letter, almost granulated in its crumpled condition, is at the visual center of the work.

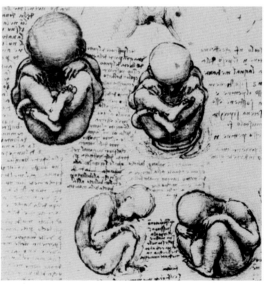

2

1. *De formato foetu*, 1626. Adriaen van der Spieghel. Printed by G.B. de Martinis and L. Pasquatus.

2. Drawings by da Vinci from his Notebooks. 15th century.

3. (and detail from previous page) *Woman Reading a Letter*. Oil on canvas. 46.5 x 39 cm. Rijksmuseum, Amsterdam.

3

Mistress and Maid

In *Mistress and Maid*, the unexpected arrival of a letter plunges the young mistress into an evident state of agitation. She is caught in the middle of writing a letter herself, probably to the very person whose letter her servant is about to hand her. Her pen stops in the middle of a sentence. Anxious and surprised, she raises her left hand to her chin seeming to scan her servant's amused and complicitous glance for some signs of encouragement.

For the first time, Vermeer ruffles the untroubled atmosphere of the house in which he sets all of his interior scenes. He is even on the verge of breaking his ever-present silence, since the two figures have their mouths slightly open, the servant hesitating

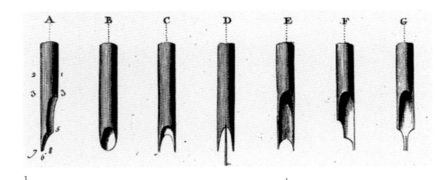

1.

1.
Different ways of sharpening a pen, taken from an illustration in Diderot's Encyclopedia.

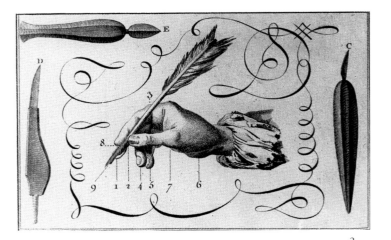

2

between laughter and compassion. A little upset in the course of love for a privileged member of the upper middle class. This is the sole disturbance the painter allows to enter into the tranquillity of the household.

Vermeer worked in the midst of the cries and laughter of his eleven children. But none of them is ever admitted into the world of his painting. Of maternity, he expresses only the silent concentration of the expectant mother. Scholars have identified three women as pregnant in his paintings. But one has to proceed with some caution. In the *Young Woman Reading a Letter* (Amsterdam*), Woman Holding a Balance* and *Woman with a Pearl Necklace,* maternity is not the central theme, and the fashion of the time (women did not wear coats, which meant that clothes were worn in layers for warmth) can cause some confusion. Vermeer's mysteriousness remains intact.

3.
Translated from French into Dutch in 1643, Jean Puget de la Serre's epistolary manual was an immediate bestseller. It ran through numerous editions.

3

1. *The Art of Writing.* Illustration from Diderot's Encyclopedia. Engraving. 18th century.

2. *The Art of Writing.* Illustration from Diderot's Encyclopedia. Engraving. 18th century.

3. *Le Secrétaire à la mode.* Frontispiece from an epistolary manual by Jean Puget de la Serre. Published in Amsterdam in 1655. Bibliothèque nationale, Paris.

4. *Mistress and Maid.* Oil on canvas. 90.2 x 78.7 cm. Frick Collection, New York.

4

1

A Lady Writing

Vermeer was able to endow his models
with what he could not provide his wife:
calm and affluence. Around 1666, he clothed
his model for *A Lady Writing* in his wife
Catharina's best outfit and adorned her with
jewelry and ribbons. The contented smile
that fleets across her lips bespeaks a sweetness of life that Vermeer and his family did
not know.

Three years earlier, Catharina's brother
Willem was arrested for beating his pregnant
sister with a steel-pointed stick. Their mother,
Maria Thins, had suffered the same treatment
from Willem's father and had divorced him
on account of it. She disinherited her son and
left his share of the estate to Catharina, as
long as Willem died without issue. To ensure
this, Maria also publicly accused Willem's
fiancé, his servant Mary Gerrits, of theft and
infidelity. Their marriage never took place.
Willem died without leaving an heir in 1676.
Vermeer had already gained the confidence
of his mother-in-law. He assumed responsibility for collecting rents owed to her and
managing her properties. The allowance
which Maria had settled on her son-in-law
and several other bequests which she made
the family were still insufficient to guarantee
a decent standard of living for a family of
eleven children.

2

2.
In this still life by Jean-
Francois de la Motte,
letters do not carry any
symbolic weight. They
are used simply to enhance
a trompe l'oeil illusion.

1. *Woman Writing a Letter* (detail). Frans van Mieris.
Panel. 25 x 20 cm.
Rijksmuseum, Amsterdam.

2. *Still Life and Trompe l'Oeil* (detail), 1677.
Jean-Francois de la Motte.
Oil on canvas. 126.5 x 93 cm.

3. *A Lady Writing.*
Oil on canvas. 45 x 39.9 cm.
National Gallery of Art, Washington.

3

The Love Letter

1

The letter at the center of this scene gives the painting its name. This little rectangle of paper, shown in contrast to the vivid yellow of the lady's jacket, has not yet been unsealed. Its arrival interrupts a peaceful morning. The maid is engaged in her housework; the mistress of the house has laid aside her tasks to spend some time playing the lute. The cushion lying next to the laundry basket, the broom propped up in the doorway, the slippers hanging in the hallway, all bespeak the calm of domestic life.

Housekeeping was practically an obsession with the Dutch. Lacking a staff of domestic servants, housewives spent most of their time engaged in household chores. A French traveler Parival, who had moved to

1.
In this painting by Samuel van Hoogstraten, there are no people, but each object has a symbolic significance. The slippers lying on the floor indicate the lovers' haste, while the broom suggests more difficult times ahead, when it will be used to chase the unfortunate husband out of the house.

2

2.
The Dutch household lent itself to studies in perspective. Emanuel de Witte abandoned for a time his favorite subject, church interiors, to explore the receding rooms in a typical bourgeois home.

Leyden, never ceased to be amazed at the Dutch "women who keep their houses cleaner than anything you could imagine. They are continually washing and polishing their wood furniture, even benches and floorboards.... No one would dare spit in these rooms, even spitting into a handkerchief is frowned upon. I feel sorry for anyone who has a bad cold."

The painters of these interiors were well served by this devotion to cleanliness. Their

1. *The Slippers*. Samuel van Hoogstraten.
Oil on canvas. 103 x 70 cm.
Musée du Louvre, Paris. RMN.

2. *Woman at a Keyboard*. Emanuel de Witte.
Oil on canvas. 77.5 x 104.5 cm.
Boymans-van Beuningen Museum, Rotterdam.

3. (and detail on following page) *The Love Letter*, ca. 1667.
Oil on canvas. 44 x 38.5 cm.
Rijksmuseum, Amsterdam.

3

canvases are groomed and polished like the floor tiles in the homes to which they render homage.

Time seems suspended. The models are mute participants in an unruffled calm. Only the objects in the room speak. None is without significance. They are as burdened with meaning as the letter itself. The musical instrument and notebook symbolize the love that is the subject of the letter; the broom and the seascape on the back wall warn us of the danger that is sure to ensue. For it is with a broomstick that one beats the unfaithful or recalcitrant lover, and the painting portends stormy weather.

1. & 2.
The contrast is striking between these two works representing the same subject: the unexpected arrival of a letter. To express surprise, Jan Verkolje has chosen agitated movement; Vermeer prefers absolute stillness.

1

Vermeer must have enjoyed bringing together so many symbols in one painting. It was perhaps his way of playing with the conventional imagery that substituted for inspiration in much of the second-rate work of the time.

Thus we have in *The Love Letter*, a parody of the genre. Nonetheless it retains its properties of mystery, stillness and silence and Vermeer's accomplished perspective. Many elements were used in other paintings of his: the satin jacket with the ermine collar, the floor tiles, the wall map from *Soldier and Laughing Girl*, which one can just make out hanging in the shadows on the left wall in the front hallway.

1. *The Messenger.* Jan Verkolje.
Oil on canvas. 59 x 53.5 cm.
Mauritshuis, The Hague.

The Letter

The prestige of having been elected syndic of the corporation of painters no doubt enhanced the market value of Vermeer's paintings. The wealthy baker, Henrick van Buyten, in whose home de Monconys had seen one of Vermeer's portraits, had not hesitated to pay 600 florins for the work. Normally Vermeer would receive between 60

2

and 150 florins for his commissioned work. During this period a pretty landscape would fetch between 10 and 15 florins while a genre scene might go for as little as 2 florins. This can hardly compare to the amount of 1,600 florins that Rembrandt received for *The Nightwatch*. By comparison, the daily salary for a textile worker was about 4 florins. Nonetheless, a painter, if he wanted to survive, had to be fairly prolific. One looks at the example of Michiel van Miereveld who was said to have executed over 10,000 portraits in his lifetime. Vermeer was a slow worker. He averaged only one or two paintings per year, and the stock from his art dealing business was estimated at no more than 500 florins at the time of his death.

Probably executed in 1671, *The Letter* is Vermeer's third work on this theme in which there are two characters. Here, there is no contact between maid and mistress. Complicity is not indicated by a look or a smile. However, the mere presence of the servant during the composition of a love letter suggests that she was in the confidence of her mistress. She has an expectant air as she looks out the window. Perhaps she is waiting for the messenger who will carry her lady's letter.

1. Molière's real name was Jean-Baptiste Poquelin.

2.
The level of public education was higher in Holland than in France. Molière pokes fun at the pretensions of the wives of the bourgeoisie in *Les Femmes Savants*.

3.
The prosperity of the United Provinces in the 17th century created a new all-powerful social class: the commercial bourgeoisie. In France, members of this class were accorded less respect. Molière lampooned them in *Le Bourgeois Gentilhomme*.

3

1. Bust of Molière. Houdin.
Marble.
Chateau de Versailles.

2. Illustration for *Les Femmes savantes* of Molière
by Joullain after Coypel, 1726.
Bibliothèque nationale, Paris.

3. Illustration for *Le Bourgeois Gentilhomme*. Molière.
Bibliothèque nationale, Paris.

4. *The Letter*.
Russborough House, Wicklow, Ireland.

4

Portraits

It was a *trone*, a portrait-bust, of Vermeer's that Balthasar de Monconys judged overvalued, when he visited Delft in 1663. Vermeer was not primarily a portrait painter. Only four portraits are today attributed to him, and there are serious questions about the authenticity of two of these. Seventeenth-century Holland could, however, claim many highly esteemed practitioners of this genre. From Rembrandt to Miereveld, passing through Frans Hals, there were numerous painters who served a burgeoning middle class, proud of its new-found success and eager to immortalize itself. The seventeenth century with its many royal families and court painters was a fertile time for portraiture throughout Europe.

Regarding Vermeer's career as an art dealer we know little. The one time he was called upon to demonstrate his expertise, it was not a matter of portraits but of twelve works purported to be by Michelangelo, Raphael, Giorgione and diverse Venetian masters. A dispute had been going on for several months between the eminent art dealer Gerard Uylenburgh and the painter Hendrick Fromentiou, advisor on art to the Grand Elector of Brandenburg, when Vermeer was called to The Hague to render an expert opinion. He confirmed that the paintings were either copies or downright fakes. Uylenburgh was forced to declare bankruptcy a short time after.

1. *Charles-Alphonse Dufresnoy, Painter.* Charles Lebrun.
Canvas glued onto wood. 73 x 59 cm.
Musée du Louvre, Paris. RMN.

2. *Portrait of the Infanta Marie-Therèse, Future Queen of France.*
Velasquez.
Oil on canvas. 71.5 x 60.5 cm.
Musée du Louvre, Paris. RMN.

3. *Suzanne Fourment.* Peter Paul Rubens.
Oil on wood. 62 x 47 cm.
Musée du Louvre, Paris. RMN.

4. *Portrait of the Artist.* Nicolas Poussin.
Oil on canvas. 98 x 74 cm.
Musée du Louvre, Paris. RMN.

5. *Hendrickje Stoffels.* Rembrandt.
Oil on canvas. 74 x 61 cm.
Musée du Louvre, Paris. RMN.

6. *Portrait Bust of Francois de Moncade, of the Netherlands for Philip IV, King of Spain.* Anthony van Dyck.
Oval. 68 x 58 cm.
Chateau de Versailles, RMN.

1

4

128

2

3

5

6

129

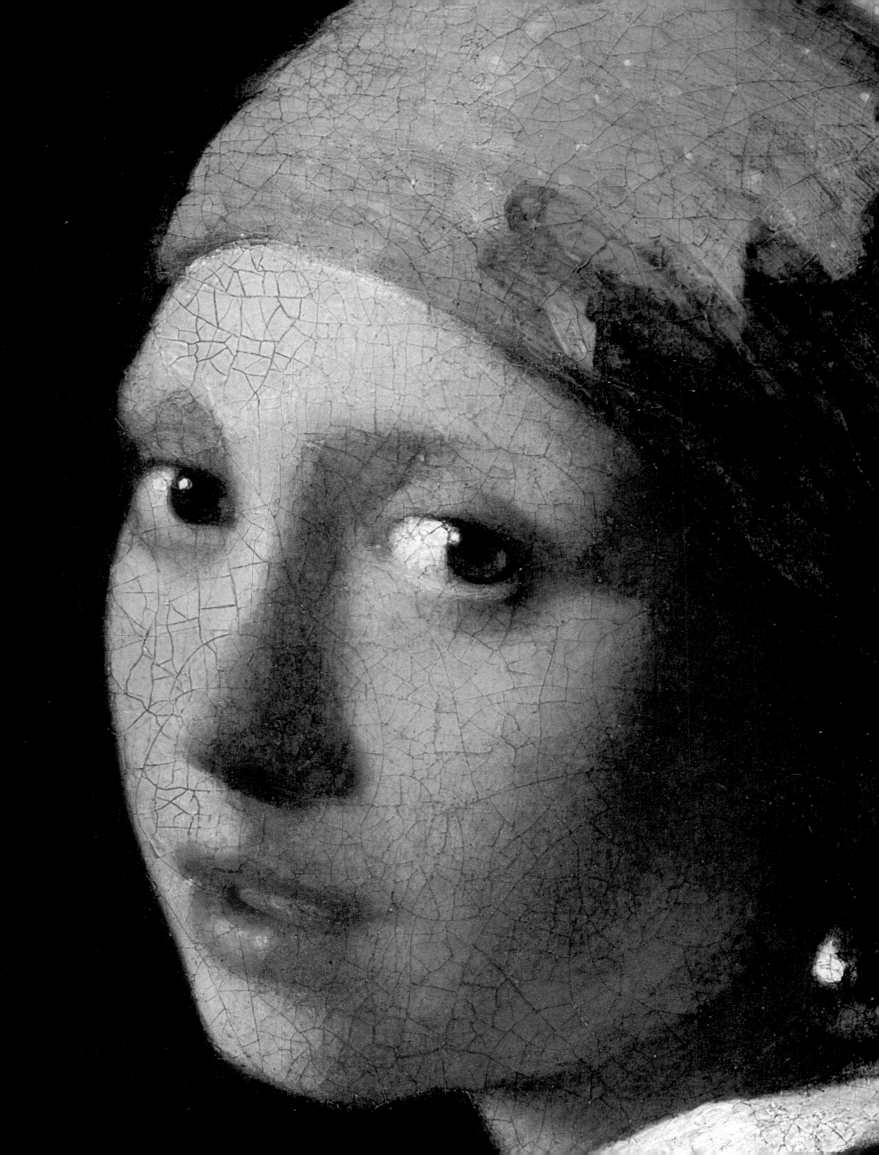

Girl with a Pearl Earring

In contrast to van Mieris, who used a magnifying glass to paint portraits of young women in very small formats with a miniaturist's technique and dexterity, Vermeer chose a format comparable to those of his interiors for *Girl with a Pearl Earring*. His painting lacks precise contours. The viewer has to step back from the canvas to appreciate its artistry. For Vermeer, the *camera obscura* was only a point of departure. The artist's genius supplied the rest.

Girl with a Pearl Earring, ca. 1665.
Oil on canvas. 46.5 x 40 cm.
Mauritshuis, The Hague.

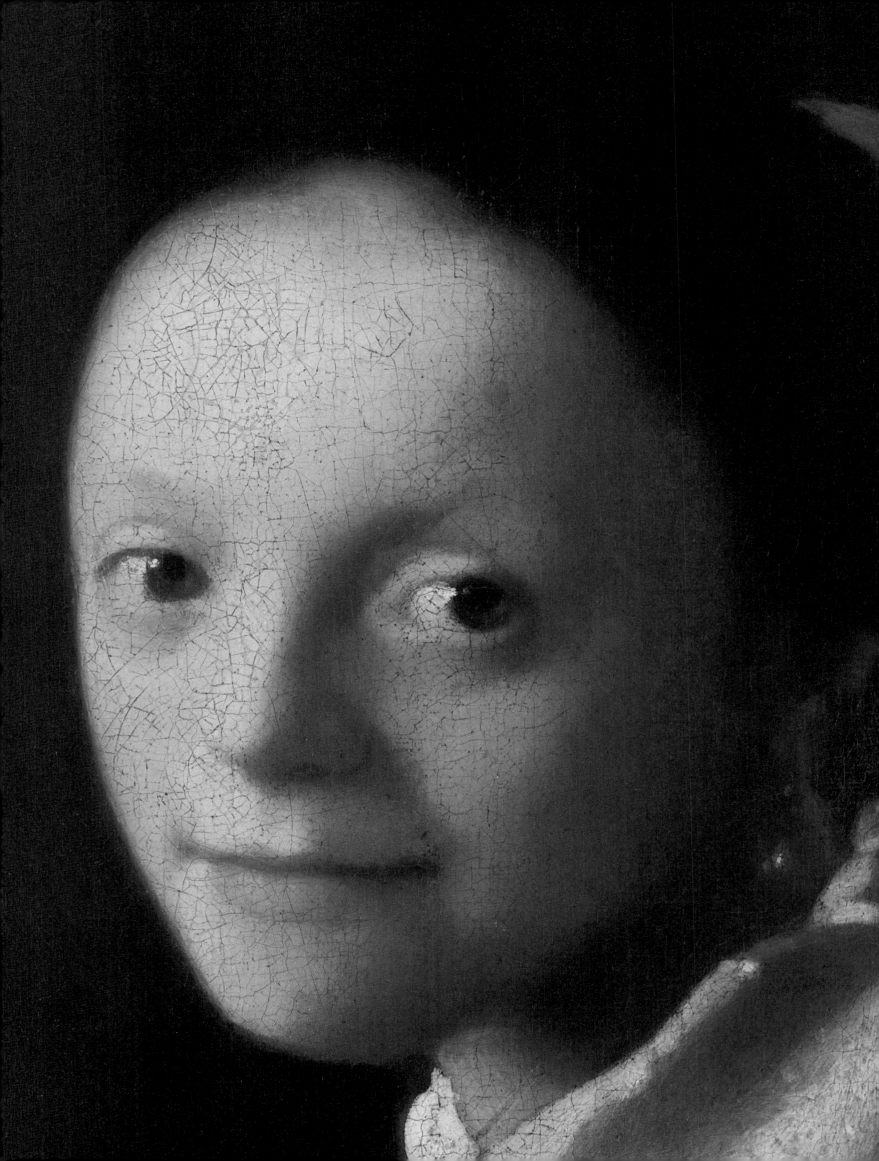

Portrait of a Young Girl

The *Portrait of a Young Girl* was probably painted with the help of the *camera obscura* as was *Girl with a Pearl Earring*, of which it is often considered a variant. Some find in the homely features of the model proof that this painting was done on commission but see it as evidence of Vermeer's ability to sweeten the imperfections of nature.

Portrait of a Young Girl, 1672-1674.
Oil on canvas. 45 x 40 cm.
Metropolitan Museum of Art, New York.

Two Recent Attributions

1.

X-ray analysis of this work
has revealed the presence
of another portrait in the
style of Rembrandt underneath
the painted surface. The position of the model is not well
defined and the lions' heads
on the chair are not oriented
to the front. These flaws
seem out of tune with the
rest of the artist's work.

1. *Girl with a Red Hat.*
Oil on wood. 23 x 18 cm.
National Gallery of Art, Washington.

2.
Attributed to Vermeer at the
beginning of the 20th century,
Young Girl with a Red Hat
and *Young Girl with a Flute*
have troubled more than one
expert. If they really are
Vermeers they would be his
only two works painted on
wood. In addition, the costumes
seem to be from a later period.

2. *Girl with a Flute*.
Oil on wood. 20.2 x 18 cm.
National Gallery of Art, Washington.

The New Jerusalem

In 1651, the Great Assembly conferred the status of a state religion on Calvinism. Calvinists adhered to biblical teachings, gave expression to their piety through prayer and defended the institution of the family. They tended toward sobriety in dress, lack of humor and distrust of the irrational. Calvinist doctrine assigned an important position to the teaching of religious texts. Its body of preachers, constituted in haste when the reform movement was just beginning to take hold, numbered about 2,000. Most preachers were drawn from modest middle-class backgrounds.

Religious diversity was, however, permitted by the law, which contributed to Holland's reputation for tolerance. But this toleration only went so far. Catholics were

1.
The Spanish painter Zurbaran (1598-1664) devoted himself to religious subjects. He painted with a gravity and austerity that was in stark contrast to the overflowing exuberance of Catholic iconography in the 17th century.

1

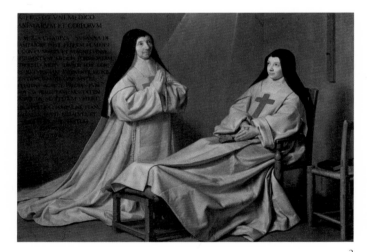

2.
The Jesuits held practically unrivaled sway over the Catholic minority in Delft. A small Jansenist community did, however, survive in the Papist quarter of the city.

2

barred from holding office and positions of public trust, such as teaching.

In 1700, there were perhaps 20,000 Jews living in Amsterdam. Excluded from the guilds, they turned their attention to commerce. In 1612, the Jewish community had built a large synagogue in the New Jerusalem, where they were able to practice their religion freely.

This coexistence between different faiths engendered remarkably little political tension. The Dutch were men of business first: Jew, Catholic, Protestant, it made no difference: the customer was always right.

1. *Saint Apollonia*, Francesco de Zurbaran.
Oil on canvas. 134 x 67 cm.
Musée du Louvre, Paris. RMN.

2. *Mother Catherine Arnauld and Sister Catherine of the order of Saint Suzanne*, 1662. Ex-voto.
Oil on canvas. 165 x 223 cm.
Musée du Louvre, Paris. RMN.

3. (and details on following pages) *The Allegory of the Faith*, 1672-1674.
Oil on canvas. 114.3 x 88.9 cm.
Metropolitan Museum of Art, New York.
Bequest of Michael Friedsam, 1931.

3

The Allegory of the Faith

Upon his marriage, Vermeer moved into the home of his mother-in-law, Maria Thins, in the "papists' quarter" in Delft. His election to high office in his guild proves that his conversion did no harm to his career. But in painting the *Allegory of the Faith* (ca. 1672), Vermeer openly ran counter to the teachings of Calvinism. Calvin had condemned papists: "They will have their chapels and their beautiful paintings, and they will fool themselves into thinking that God resides there. But He will disavow them. What else do you expect Him to do, go back on His word?" And again: "One ought to represent in painting only things that can be seen by the eye." Both the subject and composition of this painting are momentous for Vermeer, who up until this point had fled from didacticism and openly religious symbolism. Some historians have suggested that the painting was executed as a commission from certain Jesuit fathers who were acquainted with Maria Thins. The canvas does, however, avoid the overly aesthetic values condemned by the Jansenists. Its symbolic repertoire is borrowed from the *Iconologia* of Cesare Ripa, which was published in translation in Amsterdam in 1644: "Faith is symbolized by a seated women clothed in white and holding a chalice in her right hand which she looks at attentively. She rests her left hand on a book signifying Christ, with a globe placed at her feet. Under a sharp stone lies a serpent who has been trampled on. Near it is an apple, the cause of all our sin. In the distance one can see Abraham poised to sacrifice his son." For this episode from the Old Testament, Vermeer has substituted a picture of Christ on the cross. The painting of the crucifixion is by Jan Jordaen and was no doubt a part of Vermeer's inventory. The glass sphere is identified as the symbol of the human spirit in an emblem book by Willem Hesius. And while gold and pearls may not have specific symbolic denotations, they are associated with the topic of faith in numerous seventeenth-century paintings. Among other familiar elements are the tile flooring, the chair, and the globe of Jacob Hondius, which is also present in *The Geographer*.

1

2

1. to 6.

Art historians are surprised by the stilted quality of composition in *The Allegory of the Faith*. But they see Vermeer's signature in the way individual elements are treated. Substance and light are handled masterfully but perhaps the painter lacked a genuine sympathy for the subject matter in what was probably a commissioned work.

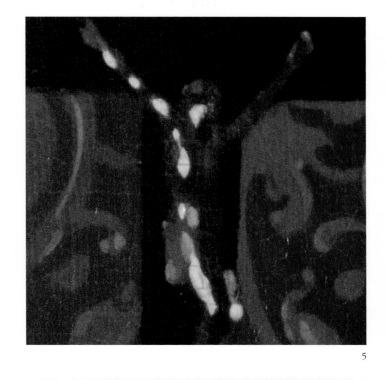

3

4

5

6

The Art of Painting

1

1.
Numerous painters have paid homage to their art. Dou, van Ostade, Berckheyde, Rijckaert and Venius opted for self portraits, Vermeer for allegory.

We never see Vermeer's face in *The Art of Painting.* He has his back turned to the viewer. His model represents Clio, the muse of History. As with *The Allegory of the Faith,* Vermeer draws on Ripa's *Iconologia* for the symbolic attributes: the crown of laurels and trumpet signifying glory and the book by Herodotus or Thucydides. One can read the objects spread over the table as symbols of the other muses: there are musical scores, books of poetry, a mask for comedy. But here the symbolism is more fluid, not cut and dried. Light circulates throughout the painting, casting each texture and surface into relief. The wall map, thought to be by the cartographer Nicolaes Visscher, who used the signature *Piscator* (fisher) is a clear yet complex reference to history. It shows "the seventeen provinces of lower Germany" but does not take into account recent political changes there. Better perhaps than a practicing historian, Vermeer registers the human cost of religious and political conflicts, and their arbitrary nature. There is a tear going through the middle of the map from top to bottom, coinciding precisely with the demarcation between the northern and southern provinces. (The north-south axis is horizontal in maps of this period.) The painter wears clothing from the sixteenth century. He is sheltered from the troubles of his time, miraculously protected from the vicissitudes of History, whose sweet face he is painting. One cannot say as much for the painting itself. It was recovered at the end of World War II from Hitler's residence at Berchtesgaden.

2

2.
The difference in these kinds of paintings lies in how the artist wishes to present his studio. Some choose to immortalize its disorder, others carefully arrange its contents to create a kind of still life. Venius chooses to show himself surrounded by his family.

1. *Painters in a Studio.* David III Rijckaert.
Oil on wood. 59 x 95 cm.
Musée du Louvre, Paris. RMN.

2. *Otto Venius and His Family.* Otto Venius.
Oil on canvas. 176 x 250 cm.
Musée du Louvre, Paris. RMN.

3. (and detail on preceding pages) *The Art of Painting.*
Oil on canvas. 120 x 100 cm.
Kunsthistorisches Museum, Vienna.

3

Of the 74 paintings identified as Vermeers by Thoré-Bürger, only 31 are recognized as Vermeers today. And eminent historians such as Arthur Wheelock and Albert Blankert have questioned the authenticity of some of these. Over the last few decades, the reputation of Vermeer has skyrocketed, while his recognized body of work has shrunk dramatically. Part of the explanation is that Vermeer was the subject of one of the longest and most fantastic frauds in the history of art. For over twenty years from 1937-1958, a forger named Hans Antonious van Meegeren fooled the most renowned specialists. In 1937, he attracted the attention of the doyen of Dutch art historians, Abraham Bredius, with a *Supper at Emmaus*, signed Vermeer. It was bought by the Rembrandt Society for the sum of 550,000 florins and became one of the most highly valued works in the Boymans Museum in Rotterdam. The same year, the great art collector van Beuningen paid 1,600,000 florins for a *Last Supper*. Three other paintings appeared on the market and found buyers as well. After the war, van Meegeren was branded as a war criminal for having sold a forged Vermeer, *Christ and the Woman Taken in Adultery*, to Hermann Goering. The forger took fright and confessed that the painting was a counterfeit. But no one believed him. Even the *Jesus among the Doctors*, which he painted for his judges, failed to convince them. Laboratory tests had confirmed that the work sold to Goering had been painted in the seventeenth century. Having worked with pigments of that era, he was caught in his own trap. It was not until 1958 that further analysis finally brought justice to van Meegeren...and to Vermeer.

1

2

1. *Woman Reading a Letter*. Hans Antonius van Meegeren.
Oil on canvas. 58.5 x 57 cm.
Rijksmuseum, Amsterdam.

2. *Mary Magdalene at the Feet of Christ*. Hans Antonius van Meegeren.
Oil on canvas. 122 x 102 cm.
Rijksmuseum, Amsterdam.

3. *Woman Playing a Lute*. Hans Antonius van Meegeren.
Oil on canvas. 58 x 47 cm.
Rijksmuseum, Amsterdam.

4. Anonymous. In the style of Vermeer.
Panel. 18.3 x 13.9 cm.
J. Bach Collection, New York.

If the forger succeeds not only in reproducing Vermeer's signature, but his style as well, than he has created something more than a forgery. (Maurice Merleau-Ponty)

3

4

Van Meegeren was not only technically meticulous in his forgeries, but also a real connoisseur of Vermeer's work. He adopted a large format for biblical subjects and a smaller one for genre scenes just as Vermeer did. It is, however, difficult to see in light of today's knowledge how these pastiches fooled so many experts. It is true that at that time a number of now discredited works had not as yet been contested.

A Painting within a Painting

1. *The Love Letter* (detail from p. 121).

Many paintings by other masters, most of which can now be identified, are shown in the rooms painted by Vermeer. The experts who have studied these "works within works" consider them to be extremely important. "Often in Vermeer, as in Jan Steen, accessories and paintings, in particular, hanging on the wall are highly significant." (Thoré-Bürger) For the art historian André Chastel, this responds first of all to a compositional need: "The regularity and authority of frontal views in Vermeer is impressive. But for this reason, pictures, maps and mirrors, so numerous in his works, are indispensable for animating his surfaces."

2

2. *Young Woman Seated at a Virginal* (detail from p. 103).

4

4. *Young Woman Seated at a Virginal* (detail from p. 103).

3

3. *Young Woman Standing at a Virginal* (detail from p. 101).

Not all of the pictures hanging in Vermeer's pictures have been identified, but it is likely that he based them on actual paintings, perhaps some that he had come in contact with during the course of his career as an art dealer. *The Procuress* by van Baburen is seen in *Young Woman Seated at a Virginal* in a gold frame, while in *The Concert* the same painting is in a black frame.

146

1

5. *Lady with Two Gentlemen* (detail from p. 52).

3

7. *Allegory of the Faith* (detail from p. 137).

3.

One recognizes in detail 6, *Moses Saved from the Waters*, which also appears in *The Astronomer*. The landscape in *The Guitar Player* is close in style to the work of Adriaen van de Velde.

2

6. *The Letter* (detail from p. 125).

4

8. *The Guitar Player* (detail from p. 91).

Vermeer's Last Years

Vermeer in *The Art of Painting* confronts History. She reveals her true face to him, which is astonishing since we know how little she intruded on his work. Historic or contemporary events play no role whatsoever in Vermeer's painting. His life exemplifies this contradiction. The artist stands outside of his time. He can choose like Rembrandt to measure his own career in a series of self-portraits, or to never let posterity see his face. It is ironic that History seems to have delivered a fatal blow to Vermeer. The invasion of the Netherlands by the army of Louis XIV in 1672, plunged the country into an economic crisis. The situation of Vermeer and his family, who were just getting by in prosperous times, became even more precarious as conditions worsened. Vermeer's election to the syndic of the corporation of painters in the capital of St. Luke was not enough to ease his straitened circumstances, and he died three years later overwhelmed by financial difficulties. He was buried on December 16, 1675, in Delft's Old Church. Catharina Bolnes, a widow at the age of 44 with eleven children to care for, described her husband's last days. "During the long ruinous war with France he not only was unable to sell his own art, but, even worse, the paintings of other artists, on which his business depended, remained on his hands. Because of this and the financial burdens of so many children, and seeing no way out of the situation, he fell into such a frenzy that from one day to another he fell sick and died." Vermeer was 43 years old.

The year before, he had married his eldest daughter, Maria, to a relatively well-off silk merchant, Johannes Cramer. The union was celebrated according to the Catholic rite at the church in Schipluy where he had married Catharina twenty-one years before.

1

1. *Young Woman Standing at a Virginal* (detail from p. 101).

2

2. *Soldier and Laughing Girl* (detail from p. 47).

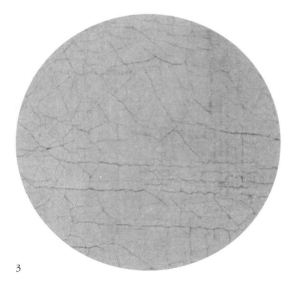

3

3. *The Music Lesson* (detail from p. 95).

4

4. *Lady with Two Gentlemen* (detail from p. 52).

5

5. *The Astronomer* (detail from p. 83).

6

6. *Girl Interrupted at Her Music* (detail from p. 107).

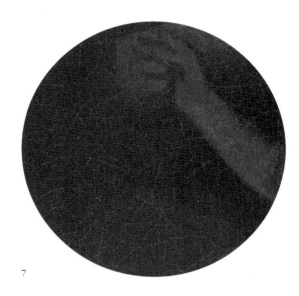

7

7. *Allegory of the Faith* (detail from p. 137).

8

8. *Woman Holding a Balance* (detail from p. 79).

9

9. *The Procuress* (detail from p. 39).

Looking at the entire body of the painter's work, we begin to become familiar with the decor in which the painter posed his models. Only details vary: the color of a picture frame, the fabric that covers the chair with the lions' heads, the motif of the tiles or the stained glass in the window. The variation is enough to prevent monotony. We know how the light at every time of day reacts with the yellow satin of the mantle bordered with ermine or the folds of the heavy tapestries. By providing us with the opportunity to see the same accessories from one painting to another, Vermeer's work allows us to imagine what his studio must have been like.

In Vermeer's Studio

1

2

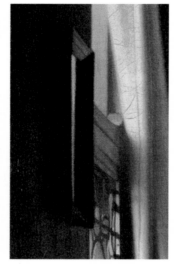

3

3. *Lady with Two Gentlemen* (detail from p. 52).

5

5. *A Girl Asleep* (detail from p. 71).

2. *Woman with a Pearl Necklace* (detail from p. 74-75).

4

7

1. *Woman Reading a Letter* (detail from p. 111).

4. *The Music Lesson* (detail from p. 95).

6

6. *Young Woman Standing at a Virginal* (detail from p. 101).

7. *The Procuress* (detail from p. 39).

9

10

8

8. *Woman Reading a Letter* (detail from p. 115).

9. *The Music Lesson* (detail from p. 95).

10. *The Music Lesson* (detail from p. 95).

11

12

11. *The Music Lesson* (detail from p. 95).

12. *Lady and Gentleman Drinking Wine* (detail from p. 49).

Vermeer Rediscovered

T wo centuries had to pass for this master's work to emerge from obscurity. It was thanks to the energy and enthusiasm of Theophile Thoré-Bürger, one of a number of Frenchmen starting with Descartes, who had sought political asylum in Holland, that Vermeer was rediscovered. Fighting tirelessly against indifference and ignorance, he insisted on recognition for a certain Van der Meer, whose works had appeared from time to time at auctions of European paintings, almost always attributed to other painters. (The names Peter de Hooch and Gabriel Metsu crop up frequently.) Fired by his discovery, Thoré-Bürger purchased for his own collection or the collections of others everything which so much as resembled Vermeer's work. At the same time, he was constantly publishing articles designed to arouse interest in the art world. The first study entirely devoted to Vermeer appeared in *Gazette des Beaux-Arts* in 1888. For over twenty years, Thoré-Bürger sacrificed everything else to his one ruling passion: "This persistent mania has cost me a great deal. To see a particular painting of Van der Meer, I have traveled hundreds of miles, to obtain a photograph I have been guilty of all kinds of follies. I even traveled throughout Germany just to establish the authenticity of works dispersed in Cologne, Brunswick, Berlin, Dresden, Pommersfelden and Vienna. And while I was hunting down his paintings, I was searching for every scrap of documentary evidence I could find concerning his life. I have gone through old books, catalogs, Dutch archives.... Concerning his biography, I still have only the barest chronological indications and a few certain facts. But isn't it said that one knows the worker by his work?"

1675.

At his death, Vermeer has only three of his own paintings remaining in his possession: *The Guitar Player, Mistress and Maid,* and *The Art of Painting.* The remaining twenty-six paintings by other masters forming the whole of his meager inventory are sold off by his widow for 500 florins. She would spend the rest of her life fighting with her creditors. Until her death, the indefatigable Maria Thins engages in numerous financial and legal maneuvers to preserve the dwindling inheritance of her daughter and eight surviving grandchildren. The debt to the baker Hendrick van Buyten, alone, had risen to over 600 florins. To the impressive collection of Vermeers already in his possession are added two or three others that are inherited by his widow.

1676.

On April 30, Catharina obtains a court order for an adjournment of debt. The illustrious Delft scientist, van Leeuwenhoek, who was born the same year as Vermeer, agrees to act as trustee to Catharina, and to work out the best terms possible with her creditors.

1695.

Twenty of Vermeer's canvases are still in Delft, in the possession of a painter on the Market Place, Jacob Dissius. Dissius had inherited these from his father-in-law, the art collector Pieter Claesz. van Ruijven.

1696.

May 11. At the death of Dissius, the greatest collection of Vermeer's works ever assembled (21 canvases) are sold at auction in Amsterdam. Some of the prices (in florins) are as follows: *Lady with Two Gentlemen*, 73 fl. *A Lady Writing*, 63 fl. *The Art of Painting*, 45 fl. *View of Delft*, 200fl. *Young Woman Standing at a Virginal*, 42.10 fl. *Woman Holding a Balance*, 155 fl. *Maidservant Pouring Milk*, 175 fl. *A Girl Asleep*, 62 fl. *Woman with a Pearl Necklace*, 30 fl. *Street in Delft*, 10 fl. *Portrait of a Young Girl*, 17 fl. *The Love Letter*, 70 fl. *Soldier and Laughing Girl*, 44.10 fl.

1749.

Alida, Vermeer's last surviving child dies in The Hague and is buried as she has lived: at public expense.

1807.

Napoleon appropriates *The Lady with Two Gentlemen* for his own collection. He maintains possession of it until 1815.

1881.

In Paris at two separate auctions, *A Girl Asleep* fetches 12,000 francs and *The Soldier and Laughing Girl*, 88,000 francs.

1945.

The Astronomer and *The Art of Painting* are retrieved from the salt mine from which they were hidden, along with 40,000 other paintings seized by Hitler, and returned to their rightful owners.

1892.

December 5. Sale of the Thoré-Bürger collection at Drouot's Hotel. *Young Woman Seated at a Virginal* goes for 25,000 francs, *Young Woman Standing at a Virginal* for 29,000 francs. *The Concert* is sold to Isabelle Stewart Gardner, who gives it to the museum that bears her name. *Woman with a Pearl Necklace*, which also belonged to Thoré-Bürger, does not figure in this sale.

1992.

The thirty-five paintings attributed to Vermeer are now all in museum collections and are considered priceless. There remain eight paintings lost or unidentified, which were mentioned either in the sale catalog of the Dissius estate in 1696, in various inventories or in auction catalogs.

Table of works attributed to Vermeer

Select Bibliography

Van der Meer de Delft, W. Bürger.
In *La Gazette des Beaux-Arts*, no. 21.
Paris, 1866

Van der Meer de Delft, H. Havard.
In *Les Artistes célèbres*,
Paris, 1888.

Leonart Bramer, sein Leben und sein Kunst. H. Wichmann.
Leipzig, 1923

Vermeeriana. L.G.N. Bouricius.
In *Oud Holland*, no. 42, 1925.

Vermeer et Proust. R. Huyghe.
In *L'Amour de l'art*, no. 17, 1936.

Thoré-Bürger en Holland. A. Heppner
In *Oud Holland*, no. 55, 1938.

Jan Vermeer van Delft. A.B. de Vries.
Amsterdam, 1939.

The Rediscovery of Vermeer. S. Meltzoff.
In *Marsyas*, no. 2, 1942.

Vermeer et Thoré-Bürger. A Blum.
Geneva, 1945.

Johannes Vermeer, Peintre de Delft (1632-1675).
P.T. Swillens. Utrecht/Brussels, 1950.

Vermeer de Delft. A. Malraux.
Paris, 1952.

Tutta la pittura di Vermeer di Delft. Vitale Bloch.
Milan, 1954.

Der Schilderkunst van Jan Vermeer. J.G. van Gelder.
Utrecht, 1958.

Johannes Vermeer (1632-1675). Gezicht op Delft.
E.L.L. de Wilde in *Openbaar kunstbesitz*, no. 3, 1959.

La vie quotidienne en Hollande au temps de Rembrandt.
Paul Zumthor. Paris, 1959.

Les Peintures de paysages dans les intérieurs hollandais du XVIIeme siecle. W. Stechow.
In *Nederlands Kunsthistorisch Jaarboek*, no. 11, 1960.

Les sujets musicaux chez Vermeer de Delft.
A. Pomme de Mirimonde.
In *La Gazette des Beaux-Arts*, no. 103.
Paris, 1961

*Johannes Vermeer van Delft (1632-1675).
Het meisje met de parel.*
J. Sjollema. In *Openbaar kunstbesitz*, no. 6, 1962.

Journal d'un collectionneur. René Gimpel.
Paris, 1963.

Johannes Vermeer, the Paintings. L. Goldscheider.
London, 1967.

La vie en Hollande au XVIIeme siècle.
Institut néerlandais/Musée des Arts Décoratifs. Paris, 1967.

Vermeer. L. Gowring.
London, 1971.

Vermeer. J. Walsh Jr.
In *The Metropolitan of Art Bulletin*, no. 31, 1973.

Vermeer: His Cartographic Sources. J.A. Welu.
In *The Art Bulletin*, no. 57, 1975.

Johannes Vermeer van Delft, 1632-1675. A. Blankert.
Utrecht/Anvers, 1975.

New Documents on Vermeer and His Family. J.M. Montias.
In *Oud Holland*, no. 91, 1977.

Johannes Vermeer 1632-1675. Een Delftse schilder en de cultuur van zijntidj.
E. van Straaten. The Hague, 1977.

Perspective, Optics and Delft Artists around 1650.
A.K. Wheelock, Jr.
New York/London, 1977.

The International Caravaggesque Movement. B. Nicholson.
Oxford, 1979.

Vermeer and His Milieu: Conclusion of an Archival Study.
J.M. Montias.
In *Oud Holland*, no. 94, 1980.

Pieter de Hooch, édition complète. P.C. Sutton.
Oxford, 1980.

Les instruments des sciences. Henri Michel.
Rhode-St-Genèse, Belgium, 1980.

La Peinture flamande et hollandaise. Herwig Guratzch.
Amsterdam, 1980.

La Faïence de Delft. H. P. Fourest.
Fribourg, Switzerland, 1980.

Vermeer. Jean Mistler.
Paris, 1981.

Vermeer's Painting Technique. A.K. Wheelock Jr.
In *Art journal*, v. 41 no. 2, 1981.

De stad Delft: cultuur en maatschappij van 1572 tot 1667.
(2 vols.)
Museum Het Prinsenhof, Delft, 1981.

Carel Fabritius. Complete Edition with a catalogue raisonée.
Christopher Brown. Oxford, 1981.

Artists and Artisans in Delft. A Socio-Economic Study of the Seventeenth Century. J.M. Montias. Princeton, 1982.

Architectural Painting in Delft. Gerard Houckgeest, Hendrick van Vliet, Emanuel de Witte. W.A. Liedke. Doornspijk, 1982.

La musique baroque de Monteverdi à Bach (1600-1750).
Manfred F. Bukofzer. Paris, 1982.

Reflets du Siècle d'or. Tableaux hollandais du XVIIeme siècle.
S. Nihom-Nijstad. Institut néerlandais, Paris, 1983.

The Art of Describing. Dutch Art in the Seventeenth Century.
S. Alpers.
London, 1983.

Spectacular Prices at Old Masters Auctions.
In *Art News*, September 1983.

Masters of Seventeenth Century Dutch Painting.
Under the direction of P.C. Sutton. Exhibition catalog from the Philadelphia Museum of Art; Berlin-Dahlem Gemäldegalerie; Royal Academy of Art, London.

La peinture de genre hollandaise au XVIIeme siècle.
Christopher Brown.
Paris, 1984.

De Rembrandt à Vermeer. Les peintres hollandais au Mauritshuis de la Haye.
Ben Broos. Exhibition catalog from the Grand Palais, Paris.
The Hague 1986.

Vermeer. Aillaud, Blankert, Montias.
Paris, 1986.

Vermeer: L'atelier du peintre. Hermann Ulrich Assemissen.
Paris, 1988.

Vermeer. John Nash.
London/Amsterdam, 1991.

Photographic Credits